OXFORD PAPERBACKS
HANDBOOKS FOR ARTISTS
General Editors: Quentin Bell and Lynton Lamb

11.   Industrial Ceramics—
Tableware

Industrial Ceramics—Tableware
Neal French

London · Oxford University Press · *New York* · *Toronto* 1972

666.68
F888i

Oxford University Press, Ely House, London W.1

GLASGOW   NEW YORK   TORONTO   MELBOURNE   WELLINGTON   CAPE TOWN
SALISBURY   IBADAN   NAIROBI   DAR ES SALAAM   LUSAKA   ADDIS ABABA
BOMBAY   CALCUTTA   MADRAS   KARACHI   LAHORE   DACCA
KUALA LUMPUR   SINGAPORE   HONG KONG   TOKYO

ISBN 0 19 289912 0

© Oxford University Press 1972

*Phototypeset by Filmtype Services Limited, Scarborough
and printed in Great Britain, at the University Press, Oxford
by Vivian Ridler, Printer to the University*

Acknowledgements

I would like to thank the following people for their help in the
preparation of this handbook:
The directors of the Worcester Royal Porcelain Co. Ltd., and the
personnel who have been so helpful not only in checking the
technical content of this book but also to me as a designer over the
past few years; in particular, Paul Gertner, George Morris,
Horace Arnold, Paul Rado and John Lance;
Henry Sandon, Curator of the Dyson Perrins Museum at Worcester
who has greatly helped me with the historical section and has
been an invaluable source of sound advice throughout;
John Beckerley and his wife, Joan, who are responsible for the
excellent photographs, reproduced by courtesy of the Worcester
Royal Porcelain Co. Ltd.—including that used on the cover;
finally, Lynton Lamb who has read and corrected my text with
such patience and understanding.

N.F.

Contents

Part III Designing

English Delft ware plate
c.. 1750, showing style of
under-glaze painting later
used on porcelain. *By
courtesy of the Dyson
Perrins Museum,
Worcester*

Preface

This handbook is intended to introduce the reader to the industry and its somewhat complicated processes from the point of view of a designer. Description of the various methods will show not only how they work but as far as possible what scope they offer a designer. Each process has its strengths and its weaknesses, a large part of a designer's job is in knowing and exploiting these.

There are four sections. The first introductory section deals with the history of the industry, in particular with the basic potting methods of the late eighteenth- and early nineteenth-centuries. This provides a background and context for the remaining three sections which deal respectively with making, decorating, and designing methods.

Introduction

Basically the methods used in making pots have altered remarkably little over the last thousand years, and the history of potting is of a gradual refinement of technique rather than of sudden revolutionary changes.

I suppose it would be fair to say that the second half of the eighteenth century saw potting turn from a craft to an industry; but even then it was a gradual and logical change of emphasis rather than of technique. It is this unusual continuity that leads me to use a brief historical outline as an introduction to this book. Not only do the current methods follow directly from those of the past — and in particular from the rationalized craft methods of the late eighteenth century — but also the present industry's not entirely healthy pre-occupation with past styles may, perhaps, be seen in better perspective.

I have been referring, and shall continue to refer, to 'the Industry' but in reality there are two industries; earthenware and china, each of which has followed a different though parallel course since 1700.

Earthenware, of unrefined red or buff firing clay, slip decorated, porous unless glazed with galena, and usually once fired, had been made in England since before the Norman Conquest.

The medieval baluster jugs and encaustic tiles, the seventeenth-century Wrotham ware, combed slip-ware and Toft chargers, all exemplify the vigorous traditions and qualities of the medium. For the greater part of this period earthenware in this country pursued its healthy way unaffected by the influences making themselves felt in Europe.

During the later Middle Ages and probably stimulated by the Crusades, trade with the East increased and specimens of Chinese porcelain began to find their way into the possession of wealthy patrons. The effect of this ware, possessing as it did all the qualities absent from the European earthenware—it was thin, hard, dense, precise, and above all translucent—must have been enormous.

There is little doubt that from the middle of the fifteenth century attempts were being made to imitate Oriental porcelain. About one hundred pieces exist of a sixteenth-century porcelain, the so-called Medici porcelain, that possessed most of the qualities of the Oriental ware, although made by totally different means. I will refer to the beginnings of the porcelain industry later; for the moment I am more concerned with the effect these influences had upon the earthenware or pottery of the time.

The potters of Europe, notably those of Italy and Spain, had for a long time been glazing their ware with an opaque white tin glaze. The ground created by this glaze was a perfect surface for painting on, and thus from the fifteenth century the Continent, unlike England, had a tradition of polychrome decoration on earthenware. The patterns used were often of Oriental origin although usually transformed beyond recognition. During the seventeenth century the Dutch potters became pre-eminent in this type of ware, almost exclusively using under-glaze blue for their decoration. It was this ware that was the first major outside influence on English earthenware.

From this period English potters started to copy the method and style of the Dutch pottery. One interesting point is that the English Delft ware centres were, like the porcelain factories a century later,

centred on ports, the places where the imported ware made its first impact: Bow, Lambeth, Bristol, and Liverpool. The main centre of earthenware manufacture, then as now in Staffordshire, remained relatively uninfluenced by the Delft ware.

Towards the end of the seventeenth century another important continental technique was copied in this country. Salt-glaze stone-ware had been produced by the German potters since the late Middle Ages. Typical of their products were the well-known 'Bellarmines', masked bottles or jugs that had persisted in scarcely altered form for hundreds of years. Now the technique was used in England but in very different style. Hitherto the earthenware, whether Delft or slip-ware, had been robust, unsophisticated, and rather roughly made. It was made for the middle and lower classes of society and considered very inferior to the pewter and other metal-ware used by the wealthier families.

Salt-glaze stone-ware made two important contributions to the development of pottery. It made necessary some preparation and blending of clays—no longer would the clay pit produce instant material—and it made possible a much more precise kind of potting, often in direct imitation of metal forms. For the first time thrown pots were turned when leather-hard, not just the bases as before but all over the outside of the pot, giving a clean, burnished finish that the thin, hard salt glaze showed to advantage. This produced, in the hands of the Nottingham potters, John Dwight of Fulham and the Elers Brothers in Staffordshire, not the hard mechanical pots one might have expected, but a wealth of fine, lively, strong, and refined shapes.

These last took the process further and around 1700 produced, by refining and modifying the local clay, a hard red stone-ware that required no glaze and could be decorated by sprigging little relief patterns from silver moulds. The Elers Brothers were much in-fluenced by Chinese stone-ware and their pots tended to have Oriental characteristics.

Far left: Nottingham stone-ware mug, 1777. Decorated at clay stage by sgraffito, impressed roller, and turning.
Left: Red stone-ware teapot, c. 1750. A late pot of Elers type, thrown and turned with relief decoration squeezed onto the pot from silver moulds.

However, the next generation of English potters in Staffordshire thoroughly assimilated the technical improvements and combined them with the best qualities of the slip-ware tradition to produce some of the finest earthenware made in this country. Astbury and Whieldon in particular produced beautiful pots turned and sprigged like the Elers ware but in buff and red clays and with soft lead glazes; often coloured to soften the effect.

This then was the situation of English earthenware at the middle of the century. The English Delft centres continued to produce until the end of the eighteenth century, though their work was of increasingly low quality. Meanwhile the potters of Staffordshire, in both lead glazed earthenware and white salt glaze, were entering a kind of renaissance.

It was at this point that manufacture of porcelain was first undertaken in this country. Since the first years of the eighteenth century, porcelain of both hard and soft paste varieties had been made at various places on the continent; broadly the German factories made hard paste and the French made soft.

Top: Worcester teapot, c. 1765. Under-glaze blue painting at its best on porcelain neatly and skilfully potted.
Bottom: New Hall teapot, c. 1795. Distinctive moulded shape and delicate on-glaze brush-stroke pattern are typical of this factory.

The terminology of porcelain is about as confusing as possible, so it might be as well to define briefly the sense in which I use the terms.

First 'porcelain' and 'china'. China has two meanings, first it is used colloquially to refer to all ceramic tableware, and secondly to refer to bone china which is itself a very specific kind of porcelain.

Porcelain is the term for a ceramic material that is vitreous, white, and translucent, and if struck will ring like a bell. It is made in a variety of ways but generally the bodies are of two quite distinct kinds. The hard-paste kind is typified by the original Chinese ware, made quite simply from china clay (kaolin), and china stone (pet-untse), raw glazed and fired at about 1400°C. Soft paste on the other hand can mean almost any imitation of the original hard paste achieved by different means. Two typical examples are the early French porcelains which are basically a mixture of a kind of glass with china clay, and bone china which is a mixture of calcined bone with china clay and flint. These both fire at much lower temperatures, the first about 1100°C., and the second at 1240°C.

In the ten years following 1745 about ten small factories began the enormously risky manufacture of porcelain in England. The odds against success were great. In the first place, the formula for the body had to be obtained, no easy matter when an established factory's success depended to a large extent upon its keeping its secrets.

Workmen, however, often proved susceptible to bribery and again there were many arcanists wandering Europe, sacked from one factory and anxious to sell their knowledge to the highest bidder. The formula once obtained was no guarantee of success either. Many were bogus and others unworkable with native raw materials. Most of the factories were set up, not by potters with a knowledge of the business, but by gentlemen-dilettanti or investors, and not amongst other potteries but scattered about all over the country. In fact the one factory set up by a potter in Staffordshire worked to such a difficult formula and had such limited success that the chastening experience delayed the major participation of Staffordshire in porcelain manufacture until the late 1780s. Finally, none of these factories was under wealthy patronage as almost all the continental ones were; the English factories from the beginning had to pay their way, while the European firms were subsidized during most of their working lives.

It seems amazing in the light of all this that any survived at all. There were, of course, many casualties, but the remainder laid the foundations for the present industry and at least one factory has been in continuous production from 1751 until the present day.

In the years between 1770 and 1810 hard-paste porcelain of a kind was made at Plymouth, Bristol, and New Hall in Staffordshire, but in the main the history of English porcelain is that of soft paste. The first fifty years were characterized by the individuality of the different factories. Although using similar techniques of making and decorating and copying each other's shapes, patterns, and marks shamelessly, the potteries still emerge as separate characters after two hundred years.

This becomes less and less true as the eighteenth century comes to an end. The factories of Bow, Chelsea, Plymouth, Lowestoft, and Bristol close and are replaced by new ones in and around Staffordshire. The many types of soft paste used at these factories die out and early in the nineteenth century are replaced by bone china as the standard and characteristically English soft-paste body. Stylistically as well, the ware becomes more uniform, the neo-classical influence produced a range of shapes predominantly oval in form that changed little from 1790 until 1830 and varied little from factory to factory.

The earthenware industry had stood very much apart from these developments since 1750. The types of ware made by Whieldon, red stone-ware, tortoise-shell glazed-ware, sprigged slip-ware, continued to be made by the next generation of potters but with increasing skill and precision. Josiah Wedgwood, of course, is the man who towers over this period but many ran him close. He had made all the types of ware mentioned above, but from 1770 developed a fine, hard, white earthenware body and produced press-moulded and thrown and turned pottery of unrivalled quality.

Wedgwood Queen's ware teacup and saucer c. 1780. Typical of the classic shapes of Wedgwood's Queen's ware, this, unusually, also has sprigged decoration. *By courtesy of the Dyson Perrins Museum, Worcester.*

Known as Queen's ware it combined considerable vitality with precision and excellence of potting unknown before. It has strong claims to be the first truly industrial pottery and was a far greater achievement than the now more widely known Jasper ware.

Wedgwood was a rare combination, a technical innovator, a sound businessman and a man with a passion for neo-classicism usually tempered with good taste. His Jasper ware, an unglazed coloured stone-ware with delicate classical sprigged ornament in white, was copied all over Europe and still is, though usually debased beyond belief. Basalt ware, also pioneered by him, was a black, unglazed stone-ware that enjoyed thirty years of popularity. One could go on; his achievements are endless; but his main contribution is that he, more than any other man, by rationalizing a craft, created the industry we have today.

By 1825 we find the china and pottery industries both centred on Stoke-on-Trent, both using industrial techniques, derived from Wedgwood and making for almost the first time similar types of ware. The classical oval teapots of 1810 were becoming the rectangular cottage teapots and as such were made both in earthenware and bone china.

During the nineteenth century more and more china factories, while still making useful ware, concentrated on ornamental pieces. It was the age of exhibitions. Each year, it seemed, there was an exhibition somewhere and each china factory had to make a show in order to survive. There was an inevitable emphasis on ornamental pieces large enough to be noticed in crowded halls, but intricately decorated to underline the factory's craftsmanship. The craftsmanship has indeed never been better than during the middle of the nineteenth century. Another result of the international exhibitions combined with a renewed interest in the past showed in a plethora of styles. Suddenly the world past and present was the designer's to plunder as he liked; textbooks on ornament showed him every style from Aztec to Louis XVI, and he used them. Incidentally, designers were an invention of this period.

Tableware was made in china during this period but generally it took second place to ornamental ware. Either it was decorated as simply as possible, to compete with the earthenware, or very expensively as rich banqueting services and cabinet services. Meanwhile, earthenware satisfied the demand for general tableware.

An interesting development at the end of the century was the production, under the influence of William Morris, of deliberately 'studio' types of ware by, among others, William de Morgan, the Martin Brothers and even by a part of the large Doulton factory.

The twentieth century has been a story of increased mechanization within the industry. The high craftsmanship of the nineteenth century has gone, more, perhaps, because of social and economic factors than anything else although unintelligent management during the inter-war period played its part. What we have now is a highly complex industry made up of hundreds of factories that differ as much in their methods as in their products. We have highly mechanized factories producing enormous quantities of ware almost untouched by hand and on the other side there are factories that are still eighteenth century in character and method.

I feel in a sense that it is impossible to talk about designing for industry: what is apt for one factory is wrong for another. Luckily, however, there is common ground. The methods of making, and to a lesser extent those of decorating, all derive from the same basic methods of the eighteenth century, so perhaps it would be worth examining them.

There have always been two main ways of making pots. The first is by *throwing* on a wheel where the shape is governed entirely by the movement of the hands as they lift and control the revolving clay. It is a method where movement is essential and where some variation is inevitable, however skilled the thrower. The second is *pressing*, where a pot is formed by a bat of clay being pressed into or over a mould, the shape being governed entirely by that mould. It is a static method and almost infinitely repeatable.

A variation of this second method, already in use in the eighteenth century, is slip-casting into a porous mould where the shape was, as with pressing, entirely governed by the mould and the thickness of the piece was determined by the casting time.

From these methods have stemmed all subsequent techniques.

Some developments were already in use in the early eighteenth century. We have already seen that the Elers brothers and the Nottingham stone-ware potters were using turning on the outside of their thrown pots. The pot, having been thrown, removed from the wheel and allowed to reach leather hardness, would be clayed down on a wheelhead and skimmed all over with a turning tool. This cleans up and refines the shape, reduces the weight of the piece and corrects the section. As a process, turning has much in common with throwing, again relying on the movement of the pot and of the hand-held tool to produce the shape.

Opposite page: Jackfield jug c. 1760. A fine example of throwing, unturned except at the foot, red earthenware with black glaze.

The next variation is different and is quite crucial in the history of making. It arose from the need to harness throwing to make repeatable shapes and consisted of the introduction of a mould to replace the outside (usually right) hand of the thrower. The method

was suitable only for small hollow-ware such as cups and bowls, but as these were the items where quantity and uniformity were most necessary this was no drawback. The revolving mould formed the outside shape of the bowl while the left hand, sometimes aided by a slate, hand-held profile, formed the inside. The bowl would not require to be turned all over its surface, a slow and skilled job in any case, but only needed to have the foot shaped by turning. Now that shapes were more uniform this was usually done on a horizontal lathe with the bowl automatically centred on a wooden 'chum' while the turning was carried out. This method, still in use and unchanged in 200 years, is discussed in more detail later in this book.

Small plates and saucers were made by an 'inside out' version of this technique. Here the mould forms the inside or top surface of the piece while the back is made by a hand-held profile. A bat of clay would be prepared by roughly flattening a ball of clay on a slate and then banging it with a heavy flat round tool known as a 'maw' until it was flat and thin enough for use. It would then be transferred to the revolving mould and pressed down by hand and sponge and the back shape achieved by the profile. Again only the footring would require any subsequent turning.

Earthenware 'Cottage' teapot, c. 1840. Typical robust, vulgar pressed shape of this period decorated with crude print and enamel pattern.

These techniques, usually called jolleying for hollow-ware and jiggering or plate making for flat, had one other important advantage over throwing as well as those of uniformity and speed. They enabled modelled decoration of a limited kind to be introduced; in particular shallow flutes, and embossed rococo decoration were used on porcelain of the time.

Pressing was carried to a very high standard of achievement during the late eighteenth and early nineteenth centuries when it became possible to make pots of complicated and irregular shape by means of plaster piece moulds. Each piece of the mould would be taken separately, a bat of clay being laid across the mould and carefully pressed into every part of the working surface of the mould with a sponge. With all the pieces complete the mould would be reassembled and the joints securely luted together and sponged; the presser would of course govern the inside shape of the pot in this way and was able to add extra clay where strength was needed and sponge off clay where the thickness was too great. It was a craft of great skill. Unfortunately, there are very few good pressers left, but to see one working is at least as exciting as watching a good potter throwing.

Pressing was used for all shapes unsuitable for throwing or jolleying, and for handles, spouts, knobs, etc.

Slip casting was the least common of these basic methods and was confined mainly to the porcelain factories, and then for a relatively short period soon after their foundation. It seems to have been the only way to make pots with some of the more intractable bodies. Thus we find sauce boats of Bristol and Worcester manufacture around 1750–5 made by casting, where five years later, when the body was stabilized, and for the rest of the century they would have been pressed. One big drawback of slip casting was that the amount of water that had to be absorbed by the mould was so great that the moulds wore out too quickly for economy. The development of deflocculants in the later nineteenth century to a great extent overcame this difficulty and from 1870 onwards casting largely superseded pressing and throwing as the standard method of making hollow-ware.

These, then, are the main methods that have persisted and which underlie all the modern techniques described in the next section.

The eighteenth-century decorating methods are also still in use but it would, I think, be untrue to say they are fundamental in the same sense as the making methods. True, the middle of the century saw the development of printing from copper plates and this could be said to foreshadow the coming of the transfer printing that is now almost universal, but in the main the hand processes of decoration, painting, gilding, groundlaying, dominate the eighteenth and nineteenth centuries on porcelain and china and to a less extent on earthenware. There, at first, clay decorating of various kinds and coloured glazes were still widely used but gave way in the early nineteenth century to printed ware, usually under-glaze.

It will be seen that the remainder of the book is laid out broadly in the same pattern as the preceding discussion of basic methods. Techniques are taken singly and explained as simply as possible.

The aim is not to enable the reader without further instruction to turn his hand to, for instance, dish-making or groundlaying. Neither is this or any other book on the subject a substitute for observing the processes on the factory floor. What it can and I hope does do is to explain the different processes, how they work and more particularly how they affect the design of tableware.

Pieces from a service made in 1802 for Lord Nelson by Chamberlain's factory. The quality and style of on-glaze painting and gilding are characteristic of the early nineteenth century. By courtesy of the Dyson Perrins Museum, Worcester.

CHAPTER 1 # Modelling

MODELLING

In the following sections, which deal with the methods used for making and decorating pottery, most will be ones that the designer knows fairly thoroughly but never himself has to use. Modelling, however, can, and possibly should be part of the designer's job. More will be said in later sections of this, but for the meantime I have thought it worth while dealing in some detail with techniques that a designer may well have to use rather than just be aware of.

MEDIA

Plaster of Paris is the medium almost universally used for pottery modelling, and while there is little doubt that in insensitive hands it has had rather a baleful influence on shapes generally, it has many advantages. It can be modelled wet or carved when set. It will not change its shape in drying—warping of models is just possible but most unusual—it neither swells nor contracts once set. It takes a good finish and deteriorates little with time. This last advantage is often essential since in normal factory practice delays usually occur between modelling and mould-making processes, delays that would normally ruin models in more perishable materials such as clay.

Clay, however, is often used, either when immediate mould-making is available or as an intermediate stage on the way to producing a plaster model. Plasticine is also used sometimes for fine detailed modelling (such as for applied sprigs) where clay presents shrinkage problems.

CONTRACTION

All ceramic bodies contract when fired, so the first stage of modelling any piece is to find out in what body it is to be made and by what method. Bone china, for example, shrinks 1 in 7, on cast-ware, 1 in 10 on jolleyed, while earthenware shrinks only 1 in 12 on cast. To produce a model for (say) a china teapot, the final fired size must be known and a linear sixth added to all measurements. This is usually complicated by the pot being required to hold a set volume of liquid instead of having to be a particular size.

To avoid too much solid geometry the usual expedient in a factory is to take as a guide for the model a mould of an existing similar pot of the required capacity. This is not only much quicker for an experienced designer but far more accurate than calculating volumes.

Lathe turning, whether on horizontal lathes or on vertical lathes or whirlers, is certainly the most widely used method for producing a model. All hollow-ware and flat-ware shapes of round section and plain surface are modelled in this way, and all pieces which will ultimately be produced by jiggering, jolleying, or any of the automatic making processes are begun by lathe turning whether or not they incorporate flutes and other embellishments.

The first stage is to prepare a plaster lump, rather larger than the proposed model. The lathe will normally have either tapering spindle attachments or stepped wooden chucks with projecting wood screws. Both of these screw directly onto the shaft of the lathe. In the former, the plaster lump is made by making a paper cone over the spindle, removing it and setting it up wide end down on glass. Around this is clayed down a cylindrical cottle of lino of the diameter and height of the proposed lump, making sure that the paper cone is central and vertical. Plaster is then poured in until the cottle is full, and is allowed to set; it can then be fitted onto the spindle on the lathe. The main drawback of this method is that the final model will have a hole running right through which must be patched when it is removed from the lathe. Also models tend to work loose while being turned, with disastrous results.

The better method is the one by which a cottle is made directly onto the wooden chuck with a step of appropriate diameter: the plaster is then held by the projecting screw heads. On vertical lathes the plaster is usually poured into a cottle made over a circular plaster bat, which is itself centred and clayed down on the wheel-head.

It is advisable to true up the lump (before the plaster reaches full

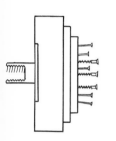

Attachments for lathe turning.

hardness) by turning SLOWLY, either by hand or power, and removing any surplus with a pointed turning tool. To allow an uncentred lump of cheese-hard plaster to revolve at full speed on the lathe is asking for spectacular trouble! The turning to shape begins with the lump trued and fully hard. There is no *right* way to turn plaster on a lathe, it is best to learn from experience. Some modellers prefer to work to an exact drawing, in which case calipers, a card profile, and extreme caution are the main requirements. This is not as foolproof as one might suppose. Pots that look convincing as full-size working drawings have a habit of looking quite different when translated into three dimensions. For this reason it is unwise to be tied too completely to drawings. One can regard turning much as one does throwing on a wheel: having established the main measurements of the model one can use the turning tool relatively uninhibited by profiles to explore the possibilities of the shape. However, this will be more fully explored later.

The main danger of turning on a wheel is 'chatter'. This is a vibration of the model that makes the turning tool cut irregularly and produces a characteristic wave pattern on the surface. It is caused by either too much pressure or using too large a surface of the turning tool to cut at any one time. When it occurs, the remedy is to skim lightly over the surface of the model with a pointed tool, and only using a chisel-ended tool when the chatter has ceased.

Turning tools deserve a comment here. I have found the most satisfactory tools are the few simple shapes illustrated, made from old files and set into $\frac{3}{4}''$ dowelling, the whole about 18" long. This length is important in controlling the tool since it must be held rigidly.

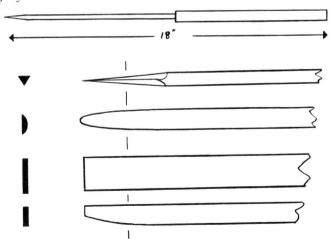

Left: Plaster turning on horizontal lathe.

Right: Turning tools.

When approaching the final shape care must be taken to avoid 'wreathing' (small undulations in the surface rather like throwing marks) which although difficult to see at this stage shows up badly on the finished pot. Careful use of a flexible metal edge will usually avert this trouble. Fine flour or glass paper produces a final finish but it tends to wear away the fine plaster and leave little pimples of hard grit upstanding if overdone.

The model is then cut from the lathe and if any further turning is required—the footring is for instance often unfinished—the piece is re-centred on a whirler, clayed down, and the turning completed.

PROFILING

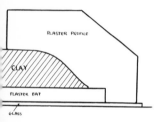

This is used to produce models when the profile is constant but the section is anything other than a circle. Oval section models are sometimes struck out on an oval jolleying machine, if the factory has one, but more often they are profiled. The method is shown at its simplest on an oval bowl. On a plaster bat of constant thickness the oval of the bowl at its rim is drawn and the bat is carefully cut a half-inch bigger all round than that oval and placed on a sheet of glass. Soft clay is built into a mound of approximately the right size on this bat and then scraped to the right shape with a plaster profile which engages as shown with the edge of the bat and the glass; it is then held at a constant angle. With care the method can give accurate results but it is usually used as the first stage in producing a plaster model of the piece. This same technique can be made to work with plaster. The bat and profile are made, as with clay; a cottle is made around the bat and plaster poured in. As soon as the plaster begins to set the cottle is removed and the profiling is done before the plaster sets hard. This requires, as can be imagined, timing, skill, and speed.

Fluting. Flutes are best cut on the plaster model soon after it leaves the lathe. The number of flutes required is decided and the model marked out. Make sure that the lines are vertical. This can sometimes best be done before the model is removed from the lathe. After it is fully marked out the job relies on the modeller's skill at carving plaster; for unless it is a cylindrical pot no profiling can be used to help him, it must all be done by eye. The more complicated the flutes are in section, the more demanding this will be; but there are no tricks. I think that as a student I expected to find, in industry, 'tricks of the trade' for all the little modelling jobs that seem impossible. There are, it is true, a few things that help; but in the main it is a question of simple methods with great patience and meticulous craftsmanship. This applies particularly to flutes; and the

16

magnitude of a modeller's job can be appreciated when one realizes that a complete range of shapes can consist of anything up to fifty or sixty pieces—many of which would have to be modelled several times—and every one of which could have forty or more flutes.

APPLIED
MODELLING Raised decoration on the surface of otherwise plain shapes can be done by modelling or sprigging directly onto the model, by moulding the plain shape and then incising in the mould or by a combination of both. Common sense will determine the appropriate method. Decoration of a non-repeating kind (of a modelled rather than a carved character) is best done direct onto the model in plasticine. Repetitive decoration in fairly high relief can be done by modelling one motive or section on glass, moulding it, and sprigging replicas onto the model. Non-repeating low relief work might be best incised into the mould; but it is always as well, when doing this, to indicate on the model prior to moulding the position and layout of the decoration. It is wise to check the incised work as one goes along, by taking clay impressions at all stages. When the relief is complete, a plaster lump is cast from the mould and cleaned up prior to re-moulding.

Moulding backwards and forwards can be used to advantage on decoration that is primarily modelled. Floral decoration, for instance, is best modelled in plasticine; but stems, stamens and the like are best incised in the mould.

The ability to break a difficult job into a logical sequence of relatively easy jobs done in positive or negative on model or mould is a prime requirement of a modeller.

Carving a handle model. Knife, riffler, and sandpaper, all shown here, are tools in what is a tricky and demanding operation.

CHAPTER 2

Mould-making

As might be supposed, the main function of the mould-making shop in any factory is to keep the potters supplied with sufficient moulds for their needs. In order that this may continue indefinitely without loss of quality, an elaborate chain of intermediate stages has to be built between the original model and the required working mould.

The first stage is to make a block mould of the model. This takes exactly the same form as the final working mould and in fact is generally used to produce initial sample pots. If the samples are satisfactory and the piece is to be put into production, the next stage is for the mould-maker to make a master, or case mould, from the block mould. The block mould having been female the case mould will be male. Each piece of the block mould is taken separately and a mould is made of it in such a way that facsimile block moulds can be produced from the case moulds. This, one might think, would be the end of the story: we now have a model, block mould, case mould, working mould and, through the case mould, the means to produce more working moulds. However, not only do working moulds have a relatively short working life before they become too worn to produce satisfactory casts, but also case moulds wear out, and one needs the means to reproduce them as well.

In practice two more stages are introduced into the chain. The case moulds, taken from the block moulds, are referred to as 'block case moulds' and are used only to produce a second generation of block moulds (working blocks): it is from these that the working case moulds are made; and in turn from these that the working moulds come. This sounds (and is) complicated; but it is essential that once a factory has started to produce an item, it should be able to continue production virtually for ever without deterioration.

Looking at the process in reverse we see that when a working mould wears out, after yielding anything from ten to a hundred pots, (depending on the body and, most important, the required standard of the ware) it can be replaced by taking more casts from the working cases. Eventually the cases wear out or get damaged (plaster is very vunerable to rough treatment), but two hundred moulds can with care be obtained from one case mould. The case moulds are replaced from the working block moulds; and usually that is as far back that the replacement process will reach. However, in the unlikely event of those *block moulds* getting worn out (or more probably damaged) then *block cases* could be used to make replacements; this still leaves the original block mould as a last resort, although this is rarely used again except for reference.

It will be seen that considerable responsibility falls upon the maker of that original block mould. Not only does the ease of production of four or more generations of moulds depend on his skill but also the quality of any future finished pieces to be made.

PLASTER Without plaster of Paris the pottery industry would not exist. Its swift setting, relatively swift drying, absorbency, and cheapness make it the only material suitable for ceramic mould-making. But it does have serious drawbacks: it is heavy, vulnerable, and has so short a working life that factories have to give up an uneconomic amount of space to mould storage. It also has a few qualities that complicate the mould-maker's job.

Firstly, setting plaster adheres to any other untreated plaster surface in the most distressing way. Soft soap is the universal separating agent; it is very effective when properly used but is far from foolproof. Whereas in other fields (plastics for example) a fairly casual wipe over with the separator will ensure mould release, the soft soap has to be applied so as to form a 'face' or impermeable surface on the very porous plaster. This is done by working the soap vigorously over the surface with a soft brush, producing a lather, then wiping this off with a soapy sponge and further wiping the surface with another sponge dipped in water and squeezed dry. Ideally this whole process is repeated three times only omitting the water sponging at the last. This produces a surface that will shed water and release plaster.

EXPANSION AND SWELL Another factor that must be taken into account is that plaster swells very slightly when setting. This is usually an advantage in making block moulds or working moulds, in that the swell tends to release the mould from its model or case; but of course when making case moulds one is casting into a female mould, where the swell tends to *tighten* the cast piece and so makes release more difficult.

Thus when the mould-maker plans his block mould he has to take into account not only the ability of the mould to release from the model when the swell of the plaster and the shrinkage of the clay are both helping, but also the intervening case moulding where release is more difficult and where care in the design of the mould is most important. As can be imagined, this is a far greater problem with figure mould making than it is with the useful ware we are discussing.

It would be impossible to describe all the techniques of mould-making so I shall describe briefly the methods used to block-mould two typical pieces: one relatively simple for machine making and the other more involved for casting.

Because a profile will form the back of the plate the modeller is only concerned with the front; and he usually will produce his model as shown in the diagram. This model has been turned on a lathe, and so will be perfectly centred. One of the most important things in moulding any piece intended for production by jolleying or jiggering, or any of the automatic or semi-automatic machines, is to ensure that the mould is perfectly centred when any modification is made to it.

The ability to centre a revolving mould by banging it with the left hand is a basic skill of mould-making. Most moulds are circular, whether destined for machine making or not, and nearly all are made on a whirler. It is a skill difficult and sometimes painful to acquire. (My own introduction to mould-making was a week spent standing at a power whirler trying to bang large sagger moulds onto centre, so that I could turn half an inch off their height. They were very heavy and my left hand bore the bruises for months.)

The mould-maker first centres the plate model carefully on his whirler and clays it down. If the modeller has left sufficient 'spare' plaster surface—about $1\frac{1}{2}''$–$2''$—outside the edge of his plate, then the model is faced with soft soap, a lino cottle is placed round it, and the block mould is run. If the spare is insufficient (and often the modeller is unable to allow enough) the mould maker builds out the model with clay to the right diameter before cottling, facing up, and pouring. When the plaster is nearly dry the cottle is removed and the mould turned true. Removed from the model, the block mould is centred and clayed down to the whirler and the 'scrapping edge' is turned on it. This is the surface that the profile will engage. Its position to a large extent determines the thickness of the plate. With this complete, the surface is once more faced up, a cottle placed around, the block case is poured and, when nearly hard, is turned up and removed from the block. Although this is the block case, it is only the front half of it. The backs of the plate case moulds are almost always made of metal, standardized so that the working moulds will fit exactly onto the platemaking wheel heads. What remains is to turn a natch or groove on the front of the case mould, that will be engaged by the projecting ring on the metal back.

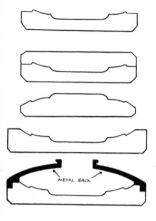

METAL BACK

Plate-moulding sequence.
From top: model; mould poured; block mould; block case shell; completed block case.

I shall use a teapot as an example of hollow-ware moulding. This, although relatively complex, shows most of the mould-making methods.

A simple round teapot without flutes will need a four-piece mould for the body, two pieces for the cover, and two each for knob, handle, and spout.

Starting with the body, the mould-maker first faces it up with
soft soap and adds short tapering 'spares' of plaster at top and bottom, as shown in the diagram. A card is then marked out with two
concentric circles, one the diameter of the spare on the foot of the
teapot and the other approximately the maximum diameter of the
pot itself. A line runs through the circles dividing them in half. Pot
and spares are then centred on these circles, and (using the points
where the straight line cuts the outer circle as centre) intersecting
arcs are drawn on the model as shown. Varying the radius of these
arcs will produce a series of intersecting lines from top to bottom of
the model on both sides. The model is removed from the card and the
intersections are connected by a line ruled with the help of a convenient flexible straight-edge. It is essential that the vertical seams
of a mould of this kind be absolutely vertical and opposite one
another: the rather elaborate procedure described above is necessary to ensure this.

Teapot model showing
position of spares and
method of marking seam
lines.

SPARES

21

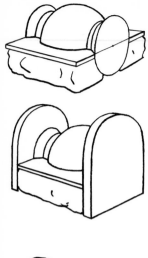

Next, the pot is placed on its side, with the seam lines horizontal. Thin plaster bats are cut carefully until they fit the pot exactly along the seam lines on either side, and are then faced up and secured in position with clay. Horseshoe-shaped end bats are placed and fixed in position and the cottle is completed by two pieces of lino fastened with cord as shown. The plaster is then poured and when it is quite set the two end bats are removed and the model turned over to show the unmoulded half. Natches are made with a natch knife, usually two on each mould face; the surface is then faced up, the end bats are fixed again, the lino replaced as before; and the second half poured. With this cleaned up, the end bats and the spares are removed from the top of the now vertical model, natches are cut in the top surface of the two completed pieces (usually two on one and three on the other to avoid confusion later) the whole is faced up, and a round lino cottle secured. A pouring hole has to be incorporated in the next piece, so when the plaster is poured and is getting cheesy, the mould (previously centred and clayed down onto a whirler) is revolved, and a square turning tool is pushed down through the centre of the mould until the flat surface inside the top of the model is reached. The tool is drawn slowly sideways until the step that forms the lid flange is reached; the tool is then angled to give a funnel shaped opening. This has to be done quickly as the plaster is setting fast. When the plaster is set, the cottle is removed and the top mould turned true, the operator taking care not to catch the turning tool in the side seams—this can be spectacularly disastrous!

From top: teapot set up in clay and bats; end bats added; cottle completed.

The mould is upended and the fourth part added, much as the third piece, but without the complication of the filling hole. The mould is cleaned up and taken apart carefully. The outside mould edges are bevelled slightly, the mould reassembled and put aside to dry.

Below left: position of natches.
Right: making the pouring hole.
Extreme right: cover moulding.

The cover is modelled separately from its flange. It is moulded by centring it on a round bat of convenient size (say one-and-a-half inches larger all round) facing both up, cottling, and pouring. The

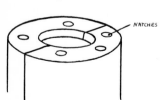

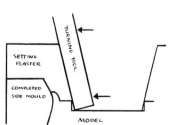

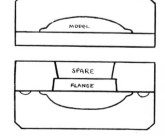

Knob and handle moulding, showing typical methods of setting.

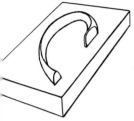

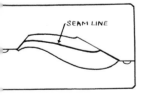

Spouts. *Above:* clay added to spout base to aid vertical mould-making. *Below:* horizontal seam mould-making.

Right: Teapot shape comparison.

mould is turned true, upended, and the flange and a large tapering spare added as shown. Natches are cut, facing up is completed, and the second half of the mould poured. As with the body mould, this is taken apart, cleaned up, reassembled, and put in the drier. The knob will usually be moulded in a two-piece mould with the seam running vertically. A spare is added to make a filling hole and a plaster bat cut (as on the body) but mounted vertically on a round bat as shown.

Handles are almost always moulded as shown in the diagram. Setting up is straightforward, using a plaster bat (as with the knob). The pouring holes at each end are usually left until moulding is complete and then cut with a knife. *Spouts* can be moulded in one of two ways. (1) A vertical seam, like the handle, has the advantage that the caster can line up the seams on the spout with that on the body of the pot, thus keeping it vertical. On the other hand, moulding this way necessitates adding clay to the sticking up area to prevent an undercut and this rather places the fit of spout to pot at the mercy of the caster's knife. (2) The horizontal seam gives a good sticking up point but no vertical guide.

I shall not attempt to deal with the intricacies of case moulding since it rarely affects a designer's job except when it gives him a last chance to change something in the modelling. This is very rarely done, since it makes the old block mould obsolete and necessitates casting a new block mould from the altered case.

It is physically possible to make moulds from almost any shape; and so in one sense the process of mould-making imposes no actual restrictions on the designer. But between what is possible and what is economically sensible lies a wide gulf, and a knowledge of mould-making methods and problems can here aid the designer. Often a small adjustment to a design can greatly aid production without detracting from the function or appearance of a piece. As a rather elementary illustration of this the diagram shows two teapots. The first (like the one described earlier) requires a four-piece mould for its body; but the second one, on account of its taper, can be produced from a two-piece mould. This would give a saving, not only on mould-making, but also on fettling in the clay state. Taking this further one could well produce a range of hollow-ware designed on the two-piece mould principle as a creative springboard.

CHAPTER 3　Methods based on throwing

In the introductory section I described jolleying as a kind of modified throwing operation where a revolving plaster mould takes the place of the right or outside hand. This is perhaps a reasonable description of the most widely used application of jolleying—cup making—but there are variations of the process such as jiggering and oval jolleying which fall outside this simple description.

There are two factors which distinguish these varied processes from the superficially similar processes in the following chapter. Firstly, that a bevelled profile (rather than a roller or 'bomb') makes the non mould-formed surface; and secondly, that the plastic clay usually undergoes a preliminary forming operation, and is not used as a slug. These I think are important distinctions.

CUP MAKING　This is the straightforward jolleying method used for small pots, such as cups, and small bowls that taper from top to bottom and will thus withdraw without difficulty from one-piece moulds. This taper need not be more than that required to make mould making possible, as explained in the previous chapter.

The sequence of making is that the cup maker first throws a convenient number of 'liners' from balls of clay (of the right weight) prepared by his assistant. A liner is a rough cylindrical pot, of the same height as the finished cup, but of little more than half the diameter. It is placed inside the cup mould and the mould itself is placed in the metal head; this is a flowerpot shaped attachment fitted on the spindle of the jolleying wheel in much the same way as a throwing head is on a throwing wheel. Jolleying heads are interchangeable and of various sizes to take the different sizes of mould, and as with the plate mould described in the last chapter, the cup mould must fit snugly into its appropriate head and run absolutely true. The cup maker draws the pot out and up the sides of the revolving mould with his fingers and a sponge pressing from the bottom to ensure that no air is trapped between clay and mould; he then brings down the profile to form the inside of the pot. This profile or template is attached to a swinging counterbalanced arm and has been set in such a way as to give exactly the right section and thickness to the piece.

The method described above is that used for making cups and bowls in bone china. With a more plastic body it is sometimes possible to use a ball of clay rather than a liner and draw it directly up the sides of the revolving mould thus cutting out an operation. On bowls larger than (say) 4" diameter it is inconvenient and unnecessary to throw liners and such pieces are formed by spreading a flat bat of clay (a process described in the section on jiggering) and then forcing it into a rough dome shape over a 'chum'—a plaster former of appropriate shape usually covered in felt. It is difficult, when using the jolleying method, to get a good crisp footring on cups and bowls made this way, since the clay resists attempts to force it into sharp corners. The usual method of making high or precisely shaped footrings on jolleyed pieces is to place the leather-hard pot on a chum of a lathe and turn the foot to shape (extra clay is allowed in the shape of the mould to enable this to be done). Advantage can be taken of this technique to give re-entrant foot shapes that could not normally be moulded. Most jolleyed pieces have to do without this refinement; and perfectly good footrings can be incorporated in the mould if they are not too deep or too sharp. Jolleying is a relatively cheap way of making pots (about half the price of slip casting on cups and similar pieces) but it has other advantages for the designer. Firstly it is an inherently strong making method less prone to distortion than on comparable cast pots. Secondly, and more importantly, it gives complete control of the section by the designer. Strength can be built in where needed to avoid either distortion in

Footrings. *From top:* jolleyed shape; turned foot; turned re-entrant foot.

Left: Cup-making, throwing liners.

firing or damage in use. Similarly a feeling of lightness can be given to serviceable pots by thinning the section towards the rim. Cast pots are necessarily of an even thickness: the inside shape is entirely dependent on the outside and often shows bad corners or stain-retaining furrows, particularly over the footring. These can easily be avoided when drawing up the section for a jolleyed piece.

Such advantages also apply to pots made by the roller method; but a jolleying profile can be altered or modified much more easily than can the expensive 'bomb' of the roller machine. This comparative flexibility makes jolleying a useful test-bed in the trial stages for pots later to be transferred to the more rigid roller machines.

PIECE-MOULD
JOLLEYING

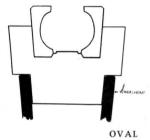

It is possible, though difficult, to jolley shapes that will not withdraw from one-piece moulds, by using multi-piece moulds and cranked profile arms. In this case the side pieces of the mould are gripped and held together by the bottom mould which fits inside the wheelhead as shown in the diagram.

The profile arm also has to be altered so it will move down into the mould, without fouling the clay, and then sideways, to exert pressure on the clay and to form the inside shape. This method is rarely used: the extreme precision and expense of mould-making normally offsets the advantages of jolleying.

OVAL
JOLLEYING

This is a more usual method: it is used in making oval casseroles. The liner is made by spreading a bat and then forming it over a felt-covered plaster chum, oval in shape. Although more difficult than normal jolleying, the sequence is the same. The maker sponges the liner into the mould on a special wheelhead, which, by an eccentric spindle, keeps the profile a constant distance from the surface of the mould. Since the strain on the clay is considerable, the method is only

Oval jolleying. The clay bat, having been formed over a chum has been placed in the mould, sponged down, and the maker has just brought down the profile to form the inside shape. Removal of the waste clay around the rim of the mould will complete this stage of making.

practicable when the finished pot is to be of a cross section thick enough to withstand it.

JIGGERING   This is the inside-out version of jolleying. Where, in cup making, the mould forms the outside of the pot and the profile the inside, in jiggering, the mould forms the top (or inside) and the profile forms the back and foot. Jiggering is principally used for making plates, saucers, and shallow bowls. As with other forms of jolleying, the operation has two stages.

In the first a slug of clay of the appropriate weight is placed on a revolving 'spreader', or flat plaster wheelhead, and is flattened to an even thickness by pressure from a flat profile. The flat bat is removed from the now stationary spreader and is slapped down on a plate mould; this is then fitted into the other wheelhead and revolved. As with cup making, the maker presses the bat down onto the mould with his hand, starting at the centre. The profile is then brought down on the roughly shaped revolving plate to form the footring and the back of the plate. Again as in cup making, this profile has been set to give exactly the right thickness and weight of the plate.

One important weakness in this process is the transfer of the clay bat to the plate mould. If the bat meets the mould off centre the spiral stresses set up in the clay by bat-making fight with the further strains induced by the profiling and result in a twisted plate. Ideally the spiral stresses set up in producing, firstly, the bat and, secondly, the plate, should have a common centre. This is sometimes achieved by introducing into the making process a third wheelhead where the bat is automatically centred on the mould by means of a plunger. One man working a machine of this type will produce about 72 plates in an hour.

Plate making. The bat is being run to the mould by pressure from the sponge and profile. When the sponge is removed the profile will give final shape to the back of the plate.

There is also the oval form of jiggering used for meat dishes, but broadly the principles are the same as with round jiggering.

Plate making. The profile has now formed the final shape and surplus clay is being removed by a wooden tool.

SELF-SCRAPPING MOULDS

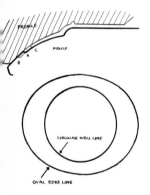

It would seem obvious that only round plates can be made by jiggering, but this is not entirely true. The footring and all the back of the plate must be round (since they are formed by a stationary profile over revolving clay) but the front and edge of the plate (formed by the mould) need not necessarily conform to the circle. In the diagram, the profile is shown forming the edge of the plate at A. By altering the mould but not the profile, the latter could make the edge at B or C, or variously between the two, as would be the effect if the plate had an oval shape but round well. This principle is used for many non-round shapes, particularly in earthenware. Such moulds are called 'self-scrapping' and are a useful departure for the designer from the round form of flat ware. But there are snags: the distance B to C should be kept as small as possible, since, because of a constant profile, as the radius changes, the height of the edge must vary, and this can cause twisting problems in firing and in decorating. This will also make you few friends among the gilders!

ROLLER METHODS

The methods which I here group together all derive from the jolleying described in the previous chapter, but with two important differences. First, instead of the stationary bevelled profile a heated revolving profile (sometimes referred to as a 'bomb') forms the inside of the pot. Secondly, instead of partially formed clay being first placed in or on the moulds, the clay, with roller machines, is used as a 'slug'.

28

This lends itself better than jolleying to automation: most roller machines now in operation are either completely or semi-automatic. The designer's problems, however, are similar. By this I mean that shapes suitable for jolleying are generally also suitable for roller making. In fact there are characteristic (though slight) shape differences in pieces made by each method from the same mould; these are referred to towards the end of the chapter.

Initial trials on a new shape are usually done by jolleying, deferring the more expensive manufacture of a 'bomb' until the shape is finalized. The roller machines are very quick, very efficient, very sophisticated, and are ideal for long runs of a particular item. Conversely they are very expensive, very inflexible, and very bad for making small numbers.

Basically there are two forms of roller machine in use. Type A (the most usual) uses a profile head or 'bomb' which contains a heating element and revolves more slowly than the mould while forming the pot. It has been found best if the profile head skids a little on the clay, to avoid a 'mangling' effect. Type B has a stationary profile head and no heating element but uses enormous force. Type A is mainly used on small and medium sizes of flat and hollow-ware. Type B is used on large hollow-ware.

Type B. The sequence is as follows: a slug of clay of the right weight is automatically cut from the pug roll and placed in the mould and the mould itself put on the wheelhead by the operator. The massive plunger carrying the roller profile descends into the revolving mould forcing the clay up the sides of the mould by sheer brute strength, a wire automatically slices the surplus clay off, and the plunger and profile withdraw. The operator takes the mould from the machine, puts it on a board and replaces it on the wheelhead with another mould already loaded with a slug of clay. To someone used to the jolleying sequence the brutal 'one shot' effect of the machine is a revelation. The drier is similarly automatic and effective. The mould on its board moves under its own weight down a gently sloping roller runway and joins a line of moulds which are slowly passed through the drier, taking about fifteen minutes. The pots are then unmoulded and with a minimum of fettling placed on boards ready for the kiln while the moulds return on another roller runway to the maker for fresh slugs of clay. With two operators, 150 pots an hour can be produced and 20 fillings can be obtained from one mould in a day.

This type has the refinement that the profile head having moved downwards into the mould, can be made to move horizontally a short distance enabling flanged hollow-ware to be made.

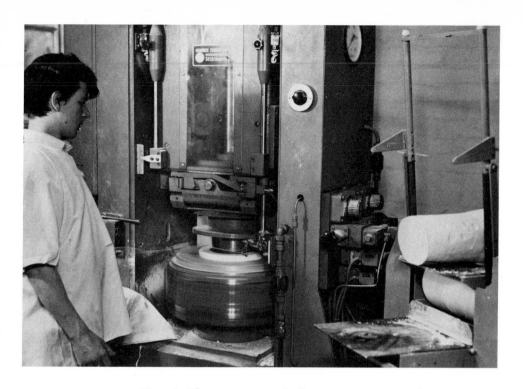

Type A. The sequence on hollow-ware is very similar except that instead of the massive plunger, as on Type B, there is a counter-balanced arm with a revolving heated profile head on one end which rocks into the mould. A turntable which can carry four moulds is often used to feed the moulds to the wheelhead. The maker puts an automatically sliced slug of clay into the mould on the turntable and the turntable revolves a quarter turn bringing the loaded mould over the wheelhead. The turntable lowers the mould into the wheelhead and at the same time the revolving heated profile head rocks forward into the mould and forces the clay up its sides. Again a wire removes the surplus. The profile withdraws and the turntable returns to its normal level and as it removes the mould from the wheelhead it turns a quarter turn on so that the mould can be taken to a drier, and at the same time it places another loaded mould above the wheelhead for the sequence to continue. One operator can produce about 180 cups an hour on this machine. Turned footrings are sometimes required (as on jolleyed ware) and this process too is built into the system. In fact turning can form all the outside surface of a cup made from a slightly oversize mould. This is particularly useful where the form of the cup makes the clay tend to crease—can-

Left: Roller making.
Type B. Bowl-making
machine in use. Plunger
is fully depressed and the
wire is removing waste
clay.

shaped cups often suffer from this at the bottom corner. Occasionally it provides the means to produce a re-entrant shape otherwise impossible except by slip-cast making. Egg coddlers are sometimes made this way, since the involved outside shape is entirely unlike the smooth inside. The thickness of section needed rules out such extremes for tableware but all-over turning is often justified, as stated, to conceal clay strain marks.

The plate-making roller machine differs mainly in the size and shape of the roller head. It does not use the turntable loading system but otherwise works much like the cup-making machine described above.

The systems I have described give a fair indication of the main types of roller machine, but each is capable of extension and refinement. Ideally the same machine, with one or two operators, could process the clay straight from pug to kiln, with automatic dryers (as on Type B), and direct loading from the towing machine onto the kiln truck. Some plate-making machines true up the slug on a separate wheelhead before transferring it to the mould; and in some cases the transfer is automatic to ensure absolute uniformity and control.

Below: Roller making cup
machine, showing four-
headed turntable. One
cup is being made, two
await removal and the
fourth mould is empty,
awaiting the next slug.

Flatware roller making, *Above:* clay slug in place on mould prior to forming operation. *Below:* Saucer being formed.

Dry fettling plates. Rough edges are removed by a metal tool, as here, and tow. A protective hood and extractor fan remove dust.

EVOLUTION

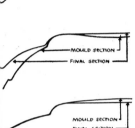

Plate making. *From top:* plate rising from mould; mould for jolleying; roller machine mould.

A clear line of evolution can be seen through these processes, particularly through the plate-making versions: from the hand-held profile; through jolleying; to semi-automatic; to roller machine, and then to completely automatic. The same mould would usually suffice for all these processes, but the behaviour of the clay on and off the mould can vary considerably. The hand-held profile is used twice during the making of a plate by that method. The first operation, immediately after sponging the bat onto the mould, forms the back of the plate. By the time the clay has dried out a little the rim of the plate will have risen from the mould and if allowed to dry out completely would result in a very much flattened rim to the plate. To avoid this the plate is forced back onto the mould by a further application of the profile.

This double profiling makes for trouble when we come to jolleying. It is less easy to organize jolleying plates, first when wet and then again when leather-hard, although it used to be and still is done in many factories. Often it would have been simpler to jolley once on moulds with very steep rims that allowed for the fall back of the plate rim, and many factories did this. Particularly in china and porcelain, not only must the mould be given a steeper rim to allow for dropping, it is also necessary to put some spring into the well of the plate to allow that to drop back flat in firing. All of this complicates the modeller's job and makes it difficult for the designer to judge plate shape from a model. But plates made on a roller machine exhibit almost the opposite characteristic. Unlike profiled or jolleyed ware the rims on roller-made plates show no tendency to drop and the centres tend even to rise slightly, so the modeller has to dish the centre of the model to achieve a final flatness. The different behaviour of clay under jolleying and roller-making methods shows up sharply in flatware; but the same kind of thing can also happen with hollow-ware, as anyone charged with converting a shape from one method to another will tell you.

One other factor that changes with the method is size. If one uses the same moulds for all three methods one can see a progressive and marked drop in size, from hand profiling to jolleying to roller making, despite the comparative stiffness of the clay.

Roller making, then, is no doubt the most important step forward in potting during this century; and it presents a special challenge to the designer. The clay, no less than when the potter throws it on the wheelhead, is a living thing to be fought and coaxed, moulded and understood.

The characteristics of each clay and of each machine have to be assimilated and used to advantage. The absence of any tendency for

33

the centre of rolled plates to drop can give the designer a chance to use a larger area than he could on jolleyed plates; and the tendency of a rolled cylinder to tuck in at the bottom can suggest a change of plane at that point. To me this kind of thing makes a nonsense of designing shapes on a drawing board.

CHAPTER 4　Methods based on pressing

Pressing, in the early nineteenth century perhaps the most important making method in the industry, is hardly used today, its place being largely taken by slip casting.

Where still found, it is largely used for small additions to pots made by another process: knobs, lugs, or sprigged decoration on ornamental shapes.

Sprigging is the simplest of all forms of pressing. The decoration is modelled on a flat sheet of glass so the simple one-piece mould has an absolutely flat surface surrounding the modelling. Clay is pressed into the shallow mould usually with the thumbs; the surplus clay is scraped off with a metal straight-edge and the pressing or sprig removed with a metal setting tool. This removal is by no means easy; the setting tool is rubbed on the flat back of the clay in such a way as to create an air seal and the sprig is lifted straight out and slid off onto a damp plaster bat prior to its being transferred to the pot it is to decorate.

Solid pressing from two-piece moulds is still used quite widely to make lugs and handles for jolleyed ware and prototype cup handles are sometimes made this way for convenience. The handle is moulded as described in Chapter 2, except that when the mould is complete and empty the mould maker cuts a V section trench on the face of the mould in such a way as to leave a sharp edge immediately around the modelling. This trench is known as a 'rigget'. The presser takes a roll of clay slightly heavier and thicker than the final handle and pushes it gently into one half of the press mould, he then puts the other half on top and presses with some force. The clay is forced to fill the mould and the surplus is squeezed out into the rigget and cut off by the sharp edge of the mould. Compared with handles made by casting, pressed handles always have a pronounced seam mark not easily cured by fettling.

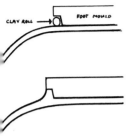

HAND MAKING

Pressing is still occasionally used in hand making dishes of a shape impossible for jolleying. The moulded section is similar to that used in jolleying and in fact the process is much the same except that the maker, having made a bat and placed it on the mould, forms the back section of the dish entirely by sponging it while slowly revolving the mould on a whirler. When he judges it to be of satisfactory section he takes a foot mould and places it in the right position on the clay press. A long thin roll of clay is pressed into the groove on the mould and smoothed into the surface of the clay press as shown. The foot mould is removed, the foot tooled smooth on the inside and mould and pressing placed in a dryer. Hand making of this kind is expensive, skilled, and has largely been superseded by the double cast method of making. However, it does give the designer the chance to create decorative flat-ware shapes too difficult in any other technique.

SLIP CASTING

As mentioned in the historical notes at the beginning of the book, slip casting was known and in use in England in the middle of the eighteenth century. It then died out, reappeared in the second half of the nineteenth century and eventually all but replaced pressing for the making of medium and large size hollow-ware.

The principle briefly is that a dry, porous plaster mould is filled with liquid clay, or slip; and the capillary action of the plaster removes a high proportion of water from the slip adjacent to it. As a result a layer of clay is built up on the mould and remains when the surplus slip is poured off. The thickness of this layer or cast can be regulated by the length of time the slip remains on the mould.

Slip casting has a very complicated chemistry which I shall not attempt to explain in any detail. However, one discovery made during the nineteenth century revolutionized casting and this I shall describe briefly. Such casting as was done in the eighteenth century was carried out using a water-slip—the clay body mixed with water to a pourable consistency. There are two main disadvantages of water-slip. The first is that the large amount of water that has to be absorbed saturates the mould, making complete drying between casts necessary, and this, together with the passage of water through the mould, radically reduces its working life. The second disadvantage is the very high shrinkage of the cast which tends to encourage distortion. The solution to both of these problems lies in reducing the water content of the slip while retaining its fluidity. It was the discovery that the addition of small quantities of sodium silicate to the slip produced exactly this result, that made slip casting a viable making method. The water content of the slip

35

could be reduced to as little as 25 per cent of that required in a water-slip of the same fluidity. Sodium silicate and the other chemicals which produce the same result are usually known as 'deflocculants'. For a full explanation of the chemical principles involved in the use of deflocculants in slip casting the reader is recommended to *An Introduction to the Technology of Pottery* by Paul Rado.

While the thickness of the cast depends directly on the length of casting time, it is fairly obvious that the rate of build-up will become slower as the deposited clay acts as a barrier. Effectively the maximum thickness of cast obtainable is half an inch. A thickness of about one eighth is, however, more usual and more efficient.

The two problems that made water-slip casting impracticable, high mould wear and high shrinkage, still affect the casting method though much less seriously than before the use of deflocculants. Mould wear tends to be much greater on cast ware than on comparable jolleyed pieces and the firing shrinkage on cast ware is sometimes half as much again as jolleyed shrinkage.

Each factory organizes the casting process differently: in some it is almost completely mechanized and in others not at all. The sequence I give here is of the stages of casting common to all.

The caster assembles the mould, making sure that the inside and seam faces are free from any old clay from previous casts. The mould is then filled with slip. Sometimes this is done while the mould revolves on a whirler with the object of eliminating a casting fault known as wreathing. Wreathing is sometimes caused in filling a stationary mould when the level of the slip rises in a series of jerks as the surface tension is broken and reforms. Use of a revolving mould avoids this but it is not altogether certain that some other

faults that occur are not aggravated by it. Casting, as you will see, is beset by even more difficulties than jolleying. To return to the sequence of casting: the filled mould is placed to one side and allowed to stand for the time necessary to produce the desired thickness (between ten and twenty minutes usually), occasionally being 'topped up' with more slip if needed. The mould is then emptied (by being upended) and the waste slip is collected for subsequent use. The mould, while draining, usually leans against other moulds, at an angle to minimize draining marks on the inside of the cast. Each shape drains differently, and some skill is needed on the part of the caster to control these marks which can look very unsightly. When the slip surface is dry the caster puts the mould again on a whirler, cuts off the waste clay with a knife and cleans up the lip of the piece. After further drying-out, the cast pot is unmoulded; and spout, handle, etc. (cast in exactly the same way) are attached to the pot with slurry—a clay/water mix the consistency of cream. What happens next rather depends on the type of body and the ideas of the particular factory. Either, at this leather-hard stage, the pot is fettled ready for the kiln with brush and sponge; or rough cleaning only is done, and the final finishing is left until the pot becomes bone dry. It is then done with tow. Either way the finishing at this stage is, or should be, of vital interest to the designer; for the pouring characteristics of teapots, coffee pots, and jugs are determined at least as much by the quality of finishing as by the design of the spout. While poorly designed spouts can rarely be saved by good finishing, good spouts are often made useless by poor fettling.

In the interests of economical making and mould making, teapots and coffee pots are often cast with spouts and handles already

p casting. *Left:* moulds ing filled. *Right:* handle ing applied. In this se it will be seen that ither pot nor handle s been fettled.

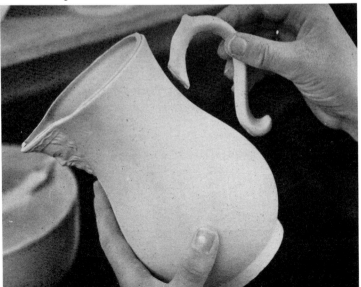

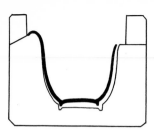

Slip cast jug with exaggerated snip hanging in mould.

attached; and if a grid is needed, it is added later from inside. This way is economical, but has the disadvantage that the cast thickness of spout and body are necessarily the same; and with the slender spouts this can reduce the bore to an impractical level. Spout thickness should ideally be somewhat less than that of the body; and a separate mould does give the chance of varying the thickness to improve the functional characteristics of the pot.

While on the subject of spouts and snips (the pouring lips of jugs) there is a problem with cream jugs and sauce boats. As the cast pot shrinks away from the mould, after the initial fettling and before unmoulding, there is a danger that exaggerated overhanging snips may hang on the mould and introduce stresses into the cast which will distort the pot in firing. The answer is partly with the designer and partly with the caster. The designer should avoid this kind of snip where possible—its pouring characteristics are suspect too— or where unavoidable the caster should unmould as soon as practicable.

DOUBLE
CASTING

Double casting is a variation of normal slip casting where both surfaces, inner as well as outer, are formed by the mould, with solid clay between. Small parts of most single or open cast pots are double, the footring for example or the flange at the top of a coffee pot. Handles, except those big enough to be cast hollow, are also double cast. But the main use of the method is for flat-ware of irregular shape, unsuitable for jolleying and where consideration of price rules out hand making.

Dishes and trays are normally filled through the footring either by having holes round the footring itself which is very difficult or with an open footring which is much easier and which confines the double casting to the area of dish outside the footring.

The difficulty with double casting is that, to avoid trapping air or liquid slip, the section of the piece must taper regularly away from its thickest point, at the pouring hole. This makes the modeller's job difficult, for while a uniform taper is relatively easy to achieve on regular shapes, these shapes are seldom the ones produced by double casting. The modeller usually produces a plaster model of the front of the dish and slowly carves the back away, constantly checking with calipers until the correct wedge or taper is achieved. Even so it is seldom right first time: subsequent work is usually necessary on mould or model or both.

From a designer's point of view double casting liberates flat-ware from the round or oval of the jolley and enables him to control both faces at least on the rim of the piece.

This is a technique which, while at the moment in an experimental stage for the making of ceramic tableware, indicates a direction in which the industry might possibly turn.

Die pressing has been used for many years in the tile industry, and is even to be found in the tableware factories for making cup rings and such. Powdered clay of low moisture content is compressed and compacted under great pressure between two halves of a metal mould. Ideal for making tiles and small, simple, solid models it is less suitable for tableware; and even such simple pieces as plates show the difficulty of applying even pressure. The plate made this way is also less dense and less strong than conventionally made ones. Tooling up costs, as well, would be very high and would rule out the method except for very large quantities.

The main advantages are the very small shrinkage on firing and the consequent low distortion, the absence of all plaster moulds, and above all the speed and simplicity of the operation. The disadvantages may be overcome, and if so the making of bulk lines such as plates, cups, and saucers could be revolutionized.

Without first-hand knowledge of the process it is impossible to say what demands and opportunities for the designer might result from this method of making. A radical rethinking of most shapes might be needed since round forms would not be easier to make than any other shapes. But the same might be said with equal truth of slip casting; and yet probably nine out of ten cast pieces are round, such is the force of tradition.

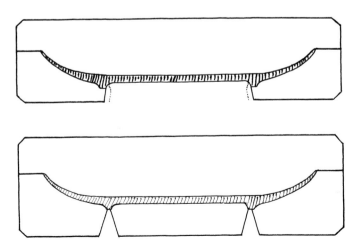

Double-cast moulds. *Top:* closed foot type, showing pouring holes. *Bottom:* open foot type.

CHAPTER 5   # Surface modelling

There are several ways in which surface modelling can be produced. The first and probably most common is where the modelling is in the mould. In this case actual decorating of the ware is carried out in effect by the modeller; all that mould-makers, makers, and glazers do is to ensure that the definition of the original work is retained as well as possible.

The modeller produces the decoration in one of three ways already mentioned: he models in clay or plasticine on the surface of the original model (or more conveniently of the block-case mould); he carves back the surface of the model or case; or he engraves or carves back the surface of the block mould.

Often it is convenient to combine some or all of these methods. For instance, a modeller working on a flower pattern might model the petals and leaves of the flowers in plasticine, get the work moulded and then engrave the stems, stamens, and other fine work on the block mould, and lastly incise the final detail on the block case. The advantages of moulded decoration of this kind lie mainly in its mass production qualities. Once modelled and moulded the ware can be produced by operatives unskilled in decoration at a cost barely above that of a correspondingly plain piece. For the designer it offers considerable freedom. Within the limits imposed by mould-making he can use whatever treatment he likes, from texture to high relief modelling. The disadvantages are twofold. Firstly, mould wear is critical: any deterioration in the sharpness of the mould shows up; so mould life is generally short. Secondly, from the factory's point of view, the modelled decoration is usually very limiting. The modelled ware must be treated as a separate shape right through the factory, creating warehousing complications; the decorating costs (calculated to cover high mould wear, mould-making, and special care in making, etc.) are built into the ware from the beginning, thus making firing losses more expensive. And worst of all, the modelling on the finished piece severely limits the number of finishes in which it can be sold, thus making it potentially vulnerable to market changes. The ideal situation, from the pottery manufacturers' point of view, would probably be to run one trouble-

Surface modelling. *Left to right:* modelling in clay or plasticine; carving on model; carving on mould.

free tableware range of a sensible shape and decorate on-glaze with transfers, patterns which would be relatively cheap to change and which would transform the rather anonymous shape into whatever style the market needed. Against this one can see just how much difficulty a modelled decoration creates. It must have a potentially long life span and if possible it must be versatile in providing opportunity for a variety of finishes.

SPRIGGING
Sprigged decoration of the kind used on Jasper ware is suitable mostly when a colour change is required or when the modelling is too high for convenient moulding with the shape. It is a skilled craft (method described in chapter 4) made more difficult when, as is usual, the ground colour of the pot differs from the colour of the sprig. Consequently, it is an expensive way of decorating and it carries many of the serious disadvantages shown by the previous method. It also allows the designer less freedom, for the pieces of modelling have to be in relatively high relief and quite compact if the transfer from mould to pot is to be workable. This is perhaps best illustrated by a low-relief floral spray. If the modelling were incorporated in the mould as in the previous method the relief could melt into the background, the stems could trail anywhere and isolated flowers could detach themselves and float in space. In sprigging none of this could happen; the relief would have to be quite high even at the edges of the spray and the stems, flowers, and leaves would all have to be massed compactly. Nevertheless, sprigging at its best has a clarity and precision never matched by the other method.

IMPRESSED
DECORATION
Roller decoration is sometimes used, mainly on earthenware and and stoneware, to give surface interest to plain shapes, usually hand-thrown. This method is that used in Leeds and Staffordshire on the creamware of the late eighteenth century, and it is still carried out in much the same way. A metal or pitcher roller, bearing a repeat pattern, is wheeled round the pot usually in a band or series of bands when the pot is leather hard. The pressure on the roller has to be very exact for uniformity, and usually such slight variation as does occur gives a pleasant hand-made feel to the pot.

Simple single motives can also be impressed on the leather-hard pot. Type-face was very convenient for back stamping one's wares in the eighteenth and nineteenth centuries, but now, when commercial and legal pressures often combine to make the back stamp a complicated certificate of authenticity, even this application of impressed decoration is uncommon.

CHAPTER 6   **Body-stain**

As the name implies, the body-stain technique involves the mixing of special colours with the clay itself.

The range of colours is limited to a certain extent by the bisque firing temperature of the ware. The source of body-stain colours, as indeed of all colours used for ceramic decoration, lies among the calcined oxides of some dozen elements. Most of these oxides are usable at on-glaze enamel firing temperatures, 700°C.—800°C. Fewer are any use at the 1000°C.—1100°C. of under-glaze decoration and fewer still at the bisque temperature that, dependent on the material, could be anything from 1000°C.—1400°C. The higher, the fewer, so body-stains relatively common on earthenware are less often found on hard-paste porcelain. However, as body-stain would diminish if not actually destroy the translucency of porcelain, it is rather an unsuitable mode of decoration for it in any case.

Body-staining can produce quite bright colours, but generally the high percentage of oxide necessary to do this makes for potting and firing side effects. The colours are particularly difficult to keep constant from one batch of clay to the next; the amount of oxide, moisture content of the clay, and pint weight of the slip are all critical, and strong colours aggravate this trouble. Consequently body-stains are pale colours generally and more often found on earthenware than elsewhere.

SOLID COLOUR   The simplest use of body-stain is where the whole pot is jolleyed or cast in the same coloured clay, body, cover, spout, handle, inside and out. A vast amount of earthenware and semi-vitreous ware is produced with no other decoration than this. It is very easy, apart from colour variation problems, and in the market for which it is aimed much more acceptable than plain white undecorated ware. The use of white clay for spout, handle, and knob is a refinement that complicates the process a little and adds to both appeal and price.

SURFACE   The price of the body-stain colour and the attractiveness of its use
COLOUR   with white have led, particularly in the fine earthenware and bone china fields, to a use of hollow-ware with an outer skin only of coloured clay, the main body of the pot being in ordinary white body. Flat-ware just has a coloured rim, thus reducing the amount of coloured clay and consequently the cost of the piece. Hollow-ware is fairly simple to produce in this way if cast. The mould is first filled with coloured slip, then emptied after a minute or two, and

42

finally refilled with white slip for the remainder of the usual casting time. Because of the simplicity and effectiveness of this technique many hollow-ware pieces are cast that would normally be jolleyed—cups, bowls, etc. Flat-ware is not so easy, but two main ways are used. The first is to use coloured slip, trailed onto the shoulder of the revolving mould—centrifugal force taking the surplus liquid clear of the clean centre part of the mould. The plate is then made over this in the normal jolleying method. The second is to sponge and jolley a thin bat of coloured clay onto the mould, cut out the unwanted centre and again jolley the white clay over the top. Considerable mould damage is apt to occur at the line of cut-off and the thin coloured bat is difficult to handle. Attempts to jolley hollow-ware are usually thwarted by the skid of the white liner over the cast surface of the coloured layer.

DECORATIVE TREATMENTS   There are a number of ways in which coloured slip can be used to produce pattern; and although slip decoration is generally thought of as the province of the studio potter it could perhaps be a useful field for investigation by designers. The following notes cover, so far as I am aware, the main uses.

Turning. A well-known type of earthenware uses this technique. Turning simple bands and rings through the blue surface coating of slip uncovers the white ground beneath. It is a simple, but very effective method of decoration, entirely suitable to the character of the ware, but necessarily confined to round pieces.

Sgraffito. As in the last method a surface coating of slip is cut away to show the white clay beneath, but in this case a freehand design replaces the turning. As a method it suffers perhaps from being associated with the 'name mug' trade.

Stencil. A rather laborious way of decorating pots, again borrowed from craft pottery, is to place paper cut-out shapes on the moulds of cast-ware before the application of coloured slip, and remove them before the white clay or slip is added. Use of a shaped stencil (made of metal foil or plastic) with the coloured slip aerographed through it seems a slightly more workable proposition, but neither of these techniques has been much used industrially.

Aerographing. Slip blown through an air brush to produce a soft graduation of colour on the mould before the piece is made is a fairly common technique, and, used intelligently, can produce pleasing effects.

Painting. Hand-painted designs in slip on the mould, either in white, before colour slip application, or in colour before white, are also possible although rarely done. Royal Worcester some years ago produced a very interesting pattern combining the first of these with aerographing.

Imitation Jasper. For over one hundred years factories have attempted to produce cheap versions of sprigged Jasper ware by using moulds with the relief modelling incorporated in them. The 'sprigged' decoration would be painted, sprayed, or pressed into the relief recesses of the mould, cleaned carefully off the background surface of the mould, and the whole then filled with the coloured slip. Either surface or solid colour gives a passable imitation of the genuine sprigged decoration, with all the advantages detailed in the last chapter that moulded motives have over sprigged ones. This again is a medium that could well be explored for its own sake rather than as a cheap imitation of Jasper; however, it is only fair to warn anyone intending to do this that the difficulties are considerable. That a technique known for over a hundred years has been so little used speaks, perhaps, for itself.

Body-stain suffers from some of the practical drawbacks of modelled decorations. Plain body-stain either of solid or surface type inhibits or restricts any subsequent on-glaze decoration and has to be treated as an extra shape in warehousing and at all stages of manufacture. To anyone unfamiliar with the working of the industry this may seem a small enough matter but warehousing, especially glost warehousing, is a complicated business. With each grade of each size of each item of each range requiring separate storage, the addition of another shape range is a move not lightly undertaken. Patterns produced in body-stain share all these drawbacks and in addition are expensive liabilities should a pattern prove unpopular, offering little chance of reclaim.

To set against these factors, body-stain has the absolute permanence of any decoration carried out at this stage. It cannot be damaged by abrasion or by acid or alkali attack; short of actual destruction of the ware it is permanent, and this increasingly becomes a cardinal virtue. There is also the less definable virtue that the decoration has a kind of 'rightness' by being part of a pottery process. It harks back in some way to the slip-ware decoration of previous centuries; and although this may be dismissed as nostalgic nonsense, I believe it is valid to consider both body-stain and surface modelling as decorating methods particularly for small and flexible factories.

CHAPTER 7 # Under-glaze decoration

A somewhat wider and certainly purer and more intense range of colours than can be obtained in body-stain are possible in under-glaze decoration. As discussed in the previous section, the number of colours available becomes smaller as the firing temperature increases. The glost temperature of most bodies used for industrial tableware tends to be less than the bisque temperature and this, on its own, increases the palette of the designer.

Body-stain colours are limited also by their necessary dilution in clay slip; and although one class of under-glaze colours also contains a percentage of clay, this serves not to dilute the colour but to make it opaque. Nevertheless the range of under-glaze colours is limited particularly when compared with the on-glaze range.

Several of the techniques used in under-glaze decoration are also used on-glaze and I shall deal more fully with them in the appropriate on-glaze section.

BANDING The main difficulty in the execution of all types of under-glaze decoration lies in the unglazed surface of the pot. High-fired ceramics such as bone china have a surface similar to cartridge paper but some low-fired earthenwares, and more particularly some porcelains, where the bisque firing is under 1000°C, show a distressing similarity to blotting paper.

Banding is perhaps the simplest and most universal way of decorating pots with a brush; it has been used at every period in all countries and seems to spring naturally from the main way of making pots. The pot is simply centred on a turntable and a stationary brush, held against the pot, makes a band of colour on it as the wheel revolves. Skill is required in this operation and it is by no means as simple as it sounds. It is especially difficult on the porous surface of unglazed pottery, for instance, not to get a load of colour where the brush leaves the pot. Again on hollow-ware, spouts, handles, lugs, etc., further complicate the task. The designer of course can help with this last problem by siting the bands either above or below the tops or bottoms of handle or spout fittings so that, when revolving, they do not foul the brush.

The porous nature of the pot surface has other side effects which need to be considered by a designer. The first is the 'one shot' nature of underglaze banding. When banding on-glaze the bander will keep the plate turning on the banding wheel until a satisfactorily smooth band has been achieved, sometimes by five or more revolutions, or sometimes by just one. If the band is still not right the whole

45

lot can be wiped off and a fresh start made. This of course is not possible under-glaze; no correction can be made and usually one revolution has to suffice. Apart from the problem of overlapping, the porosity of the ware will normally have sucked a small brush dry. Consequently large brushes full of colour have to be used to make sure that the band is completed without the brush being lifted. Also, on an abrasive surface the wear on brushes tends to be heavy. However, these disadvantages can largely be offset by skill; and good under-glaze banding has a vigour not matched by the more uniform on-glaze decoration.

PAINTING
UNDER-GLAZE
This is often used in conjunction with under-glaze banding to produce ware completely decorated and finished from the glost kiln. At best it has all its historic qualities of vigour and immediacy. The best motifs are generally simple: elaboration is expensive and detracts from the impact of the method. The more usual examples are floral, rendered by stylized arrangements of brush strokes; but there is scope for great invention. The one essential is that the motif should be painted very quickly, not only to achieve the calligraphic quality but also for economic reasons. Water-soluble gums and glycerine are the usual media for under-glaze painting.

PRINTING
We now come to what is probably the most widely used method of under-glaze decoration.

For 150 years the earthenware industry has had under-glaze printed ware as its basic product. The styles of the early and mid-nineteenth century, heavy floral borders and scene subjects in blue or brown, have likewise persisted and the taste for these shows no sign of flagging. The basic method of printing on porcelain from copper plates dates back even further to the late 1750s. This method is as follows: the ceramic colour is mixed with printer's oil—a mixture of oils and pitch—on a heated plate, and the copper with the required design engraved on it is also heated. Colour is spread over the surface of the copper and forced into the engraved design by pressure from a blunt piece of wood called a 'dabber'. Surplus colour is removed with a flat blade and the surface of the copper 'bossed' clean with a corduroy pad leaving all the engraved lines and dots on the copper filled with colour. A transfer paper is then bathed in a mixture of soft soap and water and laid on the copper. Cushioned by felt, they are then rolled together through a press, which rather resembles a mangle, once and then back. The paper, now bearing the print, is carefully peeled from the copper and passed to the transferer who trims off the surplus paper, places the

Printing. Colour being applied to the copper using a dabber.

print on the ware, and rubs it down from the back with a cloth and brush. The paper is then sponged off and the transfer is complete. This sounds, and is, complicated, although several ways have been found of speeding up the process. The roller printing machine combines all the printing part of the process into a simple continuous operation. Instead of a flat copper plate that has to be moved from place to place, from hot plate to press and back, the design is engraved on a copper roller, more difficult for the engraver but much easier for the printer. The engraved copper roller is fitted into a printing machine with a heating element inside, and revolves slowly but continuously. The printer keeps the roller supplied with colour, the surplus is removed automatically by a fixed blade, and the surface is cleaned before it comes into contact with a continuous roll of transfer paper which is fed into the machine. The printed paper is removed periodically and passed to the transferers who trim and rub the print down as in the first method. The second improvement is even more of an advance. The Murray-Curvex machine dispenses with transfer paper altogether and virtually stamps the design onto the ware, particularly flat-ware, with a carefully designed flexible gelatine pad. Here the copper is flat and it is filled with colour and cleaned off automatically before the

47

Printing. Removal of
print from copper.

'bomb' or gelatine pad descends on it, picks up the colour, and
transfers it by pressure onto the ware. The design of the pad is
crucial because it must pick up a design from a flat surface and
transfer it to a curved one without distortion or 'skid'. It is of
course unsuitable as a method for most forms of hollow-ware and
most factories use roller printing for hollow-ware and Murray-
Curvex for flat.

Printing is a method of decoration limited only by its monochrome nature and the choice of underglaze colours available. Flat
areas of colour are difficult to transfer by printing methods and are
generally more suitable to screen printing, but otherwise all kinds
of effects are obtainable. The copper need not be engraved for
instance; etching, photogravure, and other means can be used, but
the more subtle graduation of tone tend both to be lost in transferring and also to be vulnerable to wear on the copper. Copper plates
are normally coated with steel to reduce wear; even so, repairs are
necessary and the more delicate the work the more difficult the
repair. Printing under-glaze is often enlivened by the addition of
painted colour, usually simple brush strokes, to give a polychrome
look to the ware.

STAMPING Cheaper ware often has simple border patterns applied by a pat-
terned rubber roller, alternately rolled across a plate of colour and

48

around the piece. It is a very simple and perhaps crude method but it has not yet, perhaps, been exploited to the full.

Flat rubber stamps are often used for back-stamps and for simple single motif patterns. Flat shapes in sponge plastic have also been used to stamp simple patterns on ware, sometimes in combination with under-glaze painting. It is easier, for example, to do the shape of an orange by a sponge print, adding the leaves afterwards by brush strokes.

IN-GLAZE   Because of the many difficulties inherent in the porosity of the ware, a form of under-glaze decoration known as 'in-glaze' has been increasingly used recently. This is simply the use of under-glaze colours on top of the glaze, and the subsequent refiring of the piece through the glost kiln. This has the under-glaze advantage of permanence and at the same time by-passes many of the difficulties of application by the straightforward under-glaze technique.

Banding is much simpler; and more uniform results are possible on the slick glazed surface than on the rough porous finish of bisque ware.

Painting and printing are also easier; though it is doubtful whether the advantages warrant the expense of another glost firing. A technique that is more suitable for use in-glaze is 'slide off' transfer. Screen print or litho transfers in under-glaze colours can be transferred to glost ware with no difficulty, whereas they are very difficult on bisque. With increasing legislation and official sensitivity about 'lead release', it is likely that more and more litho transfer decoration (the most widely used single method of decorating pots) will be carried out in-glaze where the colours are impervious to acid attack.

With the viable introduction of screen print and litho transfer into the under-glaze decorating field, decoration is limited only by the range of colours available, by the designers' imagination, and by economic pressures. Litho is the most used and anonymous of media, capable of almost any effect but with little character of its own. However, I do not propose to treat it more fully here, since it is more properly an on-glaze method.

Most of the factory limitations of clay decoration apply also to all under-glaze decoration. Pieces lost through faults incurred in the glost kiln carry already their decorating cost. Warehousing is complicated if under-glaze decorated ware has also to have gilding or other on-glaze decoration later. However, these problems are relatively slight, while the qualities and advantages of under-glaze methods are considerable.

CHAPTER 8

Coloured glaze

The same kind of oxide stains used to colour clay can be used to colour the glaze and this in many ways is a more convenient way to get an all-over colour on a pot. As with under-glaze decoration, the colours can be much richer and much purer than when used as a body-stain. They can vary from the faintest hint to the darkest intensity, from matt to opalescent, from opaque to transparent. The range of effects obtainable by coloured glaze is enormous.

Coloured glazes are particularly effective when used over a modelled surface. The coloured glaze settles in hollows and runs thin on high points, and this gives a pleasing variation of tone that can be controlled. Designs can be modelled to take advantage of this range of tone offered by the glaze—parts required to be dark being low in relief while the light parts are high. The tendency of a glaze to run is accentuated by the fluxes in the staining oxides, so, while the decorative effect may be enhanced by this flow, it may also create problems of grinding where the glaze has run at the base of the pot.

Glaze dipping.

Pots can be given more than one coloured glaze; the most common example is when the inside of the pot is white and the outside coloured. This is achieved by first coating the inside of the pot with white glaze, by pouring some in, swilling it about, and pouring it out so that the surface is all covered. The base of the pot is then carefully lowered into a tank of coloured glaze until the glaze reaches the rim when it is quickly removed without letting any spill inside. Other arrangements can be devised. The top third or so of the pot can be coloured while the inside and remainder of the outside are white by glazing the inside, inverting the pot into the coloured glaze (air pressure will prevent colour going inside) and then completing the outside in white glaze. Some coloured glaze can be aerographed onto pots already white glazed to give a soft gradation of colour and tone; but this, like the previous method, requires great skill and control if any kind of uniformity is desired.

I feel that the main virtue of coloured glazes lies in their intrinsic qualities of colour and texture and not in the more complicated ways of applying them.

OPAQUE AND MATT GLAZES
There are successive stages in breaking down transparency and brilliance by introducing a crystalline structure to a glaze. This is usually done with tin oxide or zircon. Opaque glazes are typified by the traditional tin glaze, a milky glaze often used on red earthenware or pottery supposedly to make it more suitable for tableware use.

Matt glazes are often so matt, so rough to the touch that they can sometimes be mistaken for unglazed body. They are usually coloured and have found an increasing use in oven-ware in the last ten years. One well-known maker uses an opaque tin type glaze within and a coloured matt glaze over modelled decoration outside, with a very pleasing result.

CRYSTALLINE GLAZES
The crystal content of opaque and matt glazes is not to be confused with the crystalline glazes proper. These use not the minute crystals that give opacity, but quite different types, large enough to be seen and to have a decorative effect.

There are several constituents capable of producing crystalline glazes, notably the silicates of zinc, manganese, and calcium, and magnesium and some oxides of tungsten, vanadium, and molybdenum. The crystals are formed during cooling and require careful control of atmosphere and temperature. This, together with the high cost of the materials make crystalline glazes rather more suitable to ornamental than to tableware ceramics.

51

CRACKLE GLAZES
Here again we have a glaze effect generally considered more suitable for ornamental but with a possible application to useful ware. The effect of crazing comes from a poor body/glaze match, when the thermal expansion of the glaze is greater than that of the body. Normally, of course, this is regarded as a fault, but in some circumstances, and by rubbing colouring into the cracks, one can get quite pleasing decorative results.

SNAKESKIN GLAZE
This is the reverse of a crackle glaze. Here the body has a markedly higher expansion rate than the glaze and results in a 'crawling' of the glaze. This produces a surface of rather unpleasant texture which is sometimes deliberately induced for decorative effect. But it is less suited to tableware than either of the previously described effects.

SALT GLAZE
This ancient method (see Introduction) is still in use, but it requires special kilns and a special firing technique. From a designer's viewpoint it is just conceivable that a salt glaze manufacturer might be persuaded to make tableware; but a tableware manufacturer could never be talked into making it in salt glaze. The technique consists of bisque firing a body high in silicone content, and at about 1200°C. introducing into the kiln a salting mixture of sodium chloride and water. The salt vapourizes to form hydrogen chloride and soda, and this reacts with the body constituents to form a glaze. The use of colouring oxides with the salting mixture can produce beautiful effects.

These rather exotic techniques, although of great interest, are unlikely to enter into many designers' working lives. The most usual form of coloured glaze decoration is the straightforward coloured, glossy transparent glaze used all over the surface of the ware and sometimes over an under-glaze decoration, usually printed. Coloured glaze, also is far less limiting to subsequent on-glaze decorations than any of the previous techniques, often providing a fine background to a variety of screen print or litho designs. To a manufacturer it offers many more ways out than any of the foregoing methods and this flexibility makes it a very popular medium more particularly for earthenware.

CHAPTER 9

On-glaze painting

At one time the almost universal method of decorating tableware, on-glaze painting or enamel painting, is now ruled out by its cost from all but the most expensive ware. It is still used quite extensively in combination with engraved decoration, but even here its days seem numbered. Litho transfers can imitate most of the painting effects sufficiently well to make the expense and slowness of hand painting generally uneconomic.

Therefore when I discuss enamel painting it is less as a viable way of decorating ware than as a powerful influence on designs carried out in other media, notably in litho. At the beginning of the nineteenth century on-glaze painted decoration took two distinct forms, and these forms remain as separate influences today. The first is the kind of painting based on brush strokes where the motifs of the design are built up from the characteristic marks made by the brush. It derives from earlier ceramic painting on delft and on stoneware; and in skilled hands it combined quickness with great decorative value. The other form had the opposite qualities, it concealed instead of exploiting its means of execution, and it approached as closely as it could to the highly finished cabinet painting of the time. It was laborious, required many firings, and was expensive enough even then to make it more suitable for ornamental than for tableware.

Both styles are now imitated by litho, and it is arguable which is aesthetically the more defensible. The latter was a rather forced and inappropriate use of painting on ceramics but it has more in common with litho; whereas the former, while more acceptable as painting, cannot easily and appropriately be rendered in litho. I can offer no answer to this conundrum except perhaps to say that media and methods are seldom wrong of themselves, but only their insensitive use.

As an illustration of the continuing influence painting has on the industry, let us ask how many designers of the innumerable rose patterns in production ever take a fresh look at the flower in terms of litho techniques instead of relying on the early nineteenth century conventions of painters like Billingsley? (However, this subject more properly belongs in the litho section of the book.)

The technique of painting is nevertheless useful to a designer; for although it is rare as a production technique it is invaluable for designing on ware and for developing ideas. Methods vary from factory to factory and from painter to painter, so, although the method I describe is less than universal, I have found it simple and usually satisfactory.

53

On-glaze painting. This is small-scale brushwork painting of eighteenth century type, here used in conjunction with a printed border.

Nearly all on-glaze painting uses some form of oil medium whereas under-glaze painting generally uses water. This particular version uses fat-oil and aniseed oil, but turps, oil of cloves, linseed oil and many others, each with its own characteristics, are also used.

On-glaze pigments are invariably obtained as powders, and although these are ground quite finely by the manufacturers they will require further grinding by the painter to obtain a satisfactory smoothness. For this the colour is mixed with fat-oil (turps thickened by exposure to the air and usually prepared by the painter himself) on a ceramic tile with a pointed palette knife. The action of mixing the fat-oil with the colour results in a grinding of the colour between knife and tile and the process continues until the painter judges the colour to be sufficiently finely ground. The colour thus prepared will be rather too stiff for use and so a separate small quantity of aniseed oil and fat-oil is mixed together on a tile to a paintable consistency. The brush is worked in this each time before it picks up colour. With practice the right balance of colour to medium can be achieved for every effect. In particular, a gradation of tone from one side of the brush to the other is possible with a square-ended brush. As with so many of the techniques of the industry this is easier done than described, so I would strongly advise the reader to try for himself and find his own way. Ideally, however obtained, the consistency of the colour should give a clean brush stroke that avoids grittiness (too little medium), or fattiness (too much medium), and which shows no tendency to spread (too much aniseed oil).

Right: Raised colour. These blobs of stiff colour added to a printed design will remain proud of the surface when fired.

HAND-PAINTED PATTERNS

The few completely hand-painted patterns on the market are generally done by the eighteenth- to nineteenth-century brush-stroke method and also imitate its style. Some of the best are painted in France on English bone china plates, bone china being more sympathetic to the method than their native hard paste. It has always seemed to me something of an indictment of the English makers who claim that hand painting is too expensive to sell, that their own exported white plates (on which they certainly make no loss) can still be profitably painted, re-exported, and sold by the French.

While the shortage of good painters no less than expense makes the method unattractive to English fine china firms, painting has the one great advantage of flexibility. Patterns can be produced in an exploratory way without the initial expense of lithos. Alterations suggested by initial market response can easily be incorporated, again without the prohibitive outlay of such a rethink by any other method. The difficulty is that should the demand exceed expectations, painters will take a long time to train and meanwhile the standard or the rate of delivery will suffer.

PRINT AND ENAMEL

Colouring of under-glaze or on-glaze printed patterns by enamel painting has been an important decorating technique ever since printing on pottery was first used. The effect of simplified colouring used across the monochrome drawing of the print can be very pleasing. It is also much less demanding for painters than freehand painting and for this reason is more likely to find favour with the

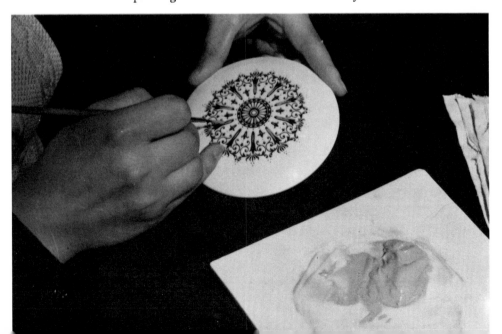

manufacturers. Its weakness lies in the ease with which litho can imitate it—much more easily and convincingly for instance than the freehand painting in the last section. In fact a number of litho patterns of the last five years have deliberately set out to use the effect of print and enamel.

TIPPING AND
RAISED COLOUR

This is a specialized kind of painting generally used with print or litho. The colours are specially stiffened so that after firing they stand up proud of the surface of the ware like jewels. To make the most of this quality the colour is almost always applied as small round blobs, often used as flower centres. The effect is very difficult to imitate on transfers so it is still quite widely used on china table-ware patterns in spite of the considerable cost.

WASH-BANDING

This is a means of covering a large area with a fairly even coat of pale colour. It is simpler, cheaper, and more direct than ground-laying (see next chapter) but is limited to pieces where, when the pot is revolved, there are no parts to foul the brush. It is ideal for plate rims and is most often used for them. The plate is centred on a banding wheel and colour is applied with a wide brush starting at the rim and moving slowly towards the centre of the plate until the area of colour is wide enough. It is extremely difficult to get an even coat and a certain amount of gradation is inevitable—even desirable.

CHAPTER 10 # Groundlaying

Another technique dating from the end of the eighteenth century, groundlaying, is still the most convenient way of obtaining a large area of flat colour particularly on curved surfaces.

The surface to be decorated is cleaned carefully to remove grease and dust, given an even coat of groundlaying oil (a mixture of turps, linseed oil, and resin) with a broad flat brush, and is then allowed to stand. When the oil has become slightly tacky it is 'bossed'. This involves the use of a firm pad 2″–3″ in diameter made from cotton wool wrapped in silk. This pad or 'boss' is dabbed firmly and repeatedly on the pot, to even out the oil over the whole surface. This dabbing is continued until the groundlayer judges that the surface has been evenly coated and the oil is sticky enough to receive the colour. The colour is exactly the same as used for on-glaze painting in its powder form. It is dusted lightly over the surface to be decorated, using a piece of cotton wool and covering the surface as quickly and smoothly as possible. The weight of colour depends on the amount and dryness of the oil; and the evenness of the coat depends on how well the oil was bossed.

Groundlaying. Dusting on the colour. The plate has been banded with oil, dried until tacky, and bossed smooth. Powdered colour is now being applied to it with cotton wool to give a flat even ground.

This is a skilled craft, and a good groundlayer must be able to judge his bossing to give absolute uniformity for any particular pattern over long periods of time and with changing atmosphere and temperature. For solid covering in a rich colour, ruby for example, it is usual to give one fairly light coat, then fire it in before building up to the final strength with another application. As well as obtaining a richness difficult to achieve in one coat this makes uniformity across a range of pieces rather more easy.

The dabbing tends to spread the oil beyond the area to be ground-laid and when dusting is complete the limits of the groundlay have to be defined and the surplus colour removed. Powdered ceramic colour has a knack of getting everywhere, and unless every speck is removed before firing the result will be a very expensively produced piece of seconds china. The cleaning is done with cotton wool but a clean edge is first given to the groundlay, often with a piece of sharpened wood—a paintbrush handle is ideal. On circular pots, where the groundlay takes the form of a band, this is done by centring the pot on a banding wheel, revolving it, applying the wood to the groundlay and scratching through it in a line about one-eighth of an inch wide either side of the band. It is then easy to clean off the unwanted colour leaving a precise and even groundlaid band.

Where the edge of the groundlay is curved or has a decorative shape, a template is used to aid cleaning off, or stencilling is employed. This rather elaborate method is only feasible on the most expensive patterns because of its slowness and high cost. An outline of the required shape is printed on the ware and fired, then, before groundlaying, a mixture of glucose and water is painted on the piece up to and outside the line. When this is dry, groundlaying is carried out in the normal way and is allowed to stand for some hours. When the ground is hard the ware is immersed in water and the surplus colour floats off.

Oil of cloves or Brunswick black are also sometimes used to aid cleaning off. Both have the effect of softening the hardened groundlay oil and, when painted over unfired groundlaid colour that has been allowed to stand, enable the groundlayer to wipe off precise areas of colour without any preliminary scratching round with a pointed stick.

Groundlay is almost invariably used in conjuction with other decorating methods: gilding, printing, painting, or litho; and of course on expensive ware. The flatness of groundlaid colour has led to its use by designers to imitate screen printed designs—very laborious but useful—as a way of producing convincing sample pieces. I shall refer to this in the section on design methods.

CHAPTER 11 **Printing**

In the section on under-glaze decoration is a fairly detailed account of colour printing so here I shall deal with the other aspects and versions of printing.

ENGRAVING Although eighteenth-century copper plates were usually etched, the next century saw the introduction and use in ceramics of engraving, and the designs on most coppers today are arrived at by this method. Basically engraving uses two methods and two kinds of tool. Cutting is the first method, and for this a graver is used. Punching is the second, and for this hammer and punch are the tools.

The design to be cut is transferred to the copper either by photography, or by the engraver tracing or copying from the original design. The copper is placed on a pad and the engraver cuts the

Engraving. A small-scale pattern is here being cut using a graver.

design using graver for line and hatched tone and the punch where softer gradations of tone are needed. I have talked much about skills through this book and it is an industry richer in manual skills than most but none is more demanding, precise, and difficult to acquire than that of engraving. As examples of fine engraving I show part of one design carried out almost entirely by punching, and another using mainly line. The extreme control of tone across the modelled areas and the precision of line on both show engraving at its very best.

When the engraving is complete, the engraver takes off trial prints. Areas that prove to be too light can be re-worked and areas that are too dark can be rubbed down. Any alterations are made by punching the copper up from the back using a blunt-ended round punch, stoning it flat again on the front and carrying out the desired work. This of course is only possible on flat coppers. Before being used for production the copper is normally sent away to be steel-plated, a process that prolongs its working life greatly. However, it will still require in time to be recut and a great deal of engraver's time, particularly that of engravers working on a factory (as opposed to those working in independent studios) is taken up with repairing engraved plates. It is useful training for apprentice engravers, and a necessary stage before they are allowed to cut fresh copper plates.

Some pottery factories still have their own engraving shops but more and more work is being done by independent studios. In some ways this may have kept the general standards of engraving higher, but the presence of good engravers and good engraved decoration on a factory usually exerts a beneficial influence on its design generally.

Engraving. *Above:* this pattern shows the characteristic subtle gradations of tone obtained by fine punching. *Below:* this in contrast shows the power of line engraving using a graver.

<table>
<tr>
<td>PHOTO
ETCHING</td>
<td>Of the other methods of preparing coppers photo etching is the most usual. It is a process invariably carried out off the factory and in essence is as follows. The copper is evenly coated with an acid resist and then exposed to a photographic positive image of the design. The light softens the resist when it touches it and the softened resist is washed off. The back and side surfaces of the copper are covered in resist and the whole area exposed to acid fumes. The design is thus bitten into the copper and is ready for use. The method has none of the real virtues of engraving and in many ways more resembles a one-colour litho; however, for some kinds of effect it is useful.</td>
</tr>
<tr>
<td>GOLD
PRINTING</td>
<td>This is carried out in one of two ways. It can be treated as any other colour, mixed with the printer's oil, and printed directly as already described. Or the pattern can be transferred in oil or varnish onto the ware and the gold dusted on in powder form. Both methods are in common use and it seems largely a matter of factory usage as to which is employed.</td>
</tr>
<tr>
<td>RAISED PASTE
PRINTING</td>
<td>This method of decoration stems from the second of the alternative methods of gold printing mentioned above. The object is to produce an engraved pattern in gold where the design stands proud of the surface, giving a filigree or even an encrusted look to the piece.</td>
</tr>
</table>

This is obtained firstly and naturally enough by engraving the design in the copper more deeply than usual. Then, instead of printing in gold, the design is printed in paste. This is a substance made of tin oxide, zinc oxide, antimony, borax, China clay, Cornish stone and flint which when fired keeps its shape, adheres firmly to the glaze, and is slightly porous. After the piece has been printed in raised paste and enamel fired at 740°C. it is coated with a mixture of turps and printing oil and then the surface is wiped clean and dry. The raised paste being porous will have retained some oil, so when gold dust is brushed across the surface it adheres only to the raised design. After cleaning, the piece is fired once more at gold tempera-ture (740°C.), and after burnishing the characteristic filigree look appears. It is, needless to say, very expensive and has now largely been superseded by two silk-screen developments. First it became possible to transfer the raised paste by slide off transfers produced by silk screen, thus cutting out the difficult printing operation. Then a way was found to transfer gold and paste together, cutting out printing, dusting, and one firing. The transfer prints are expen-sive, but much less so than the original process which is less and less used.

This process uses the thickness of the glaze on china (like the last process it is seldom used on anything but bone china) to give a rich effect to bands of gold. The idea is that a design is bitten into the surface of the glaze and when gold is banded over this, fired, and burnished, the bitten areas stay dull and matt while the areas still raised are brilliantly polished.

This is achieved by printing the design, almost always a narrow band around the edge of plates and hollow-ware, not in colour but in a wax resist. The printed pattern, being that required to be raised at the final stage, is transferred in the normal way. Then the piece is painted all over, inside and out, with more resist, usually Brunswick black, in such a way that apart from the white areas within the pattern no part of the pot is unprotected. It is then immersed in hydrofluoric acid for a few minutes. The dipping time of course is critical—too little and the design will be too faint, too long and the acid will be right through the glaze and the gold will not take. The ideal bite is half-way through the glaze but this is difficult to achieve when the glaze thickness tends to be variable. The plate is washed in water, soda, and then water again to ensure that none of the very powerful acid is allowed to escape. It next goes to the gilders for a band of gold to be applied over the bitten design and is then fired. A further application of gold and a further firing are necessary in most cases to give a solid coat, and then the piece is burnished. The full effect is only obtained by burnishing the piece with a bloodstone which leaves the recessed parts of the design matt as from the kiln while imparting a brilliant polish to the surface. This is slow and costly, however, and although the whole process is very expensive it has recently been thought worth saving a little of the cost by sand-burnishing instead. This burnishes the surface less brilliantly and the recessed parts almost as much, and so a quite different effect is produced.

Acid etching. Blacking-out with resist. The printed resist pattern is seen at the shoulder of the piece.

Cheaper imitations of the acid etching technique have recently been developed as they have been for raised paste printing. Silk-screen raised patterns underneath a gold band give something of the general effect of acid etching, particularly of the sanded kind, but they seem unlikely to replace it entirely.

CHAPTER 12

Transfer printing

Transfer prints produced by lithography and by screen printing are now the almost universal way of decorating pottery throughout the industry. The invention of lithographic transfer prints towards the end of the last century revolutionized ceramic decoration. Suddenly complicated polychromatic effects formerly only obtainable by expensive hand painting were put within the reach of the makers of lower-priced ware. More significantly, decoration formerly produced in the small quantities necessitated by the slowness of hand work now could be made in large quantities, and also, because of the economics of transfer printing, had to be produced in large quantities. Once litho plates for a design have been prepared, the press set up, and the colours prepared, the more prints a litho manufacturer produces the cheaper each one will be. From this it can be seen that the onus is on the pottery manufacturer to find a design of universal appeal and then to flood the market with it. This is true of other methods of decoration of course, but applies in particular to transfer printing which is almost the only area of pottery making and decorating where the most significant part of the process is done by a specialist manufacturer off the factory.

This has led to a further departure. The transfer manufacturer has his own staff of designers who produce patterns for sale to the industry, either exclusively to one firm or in open stock to whoever wants it. Formerly, decorations were evolved entirely within a factory, interpreting the current style in terms of the methods and craftsmen available at that factory. Now we have a situation where the factory merely chooses a pattern off the shelf from the litho or screen-print manufacturer. This has not surprisingly had a great levelling effect across the industry.

There are, however, still many companies who produce their own designs for transfer prints and I shall have more to say later about the designer's part in the preparation of designs and fittings for litho and screen print. For the moment it is only necessary to say that

the design is usually carried out on paper and passed to the manufacturer.

What eventually comes back (when the fittings, sizes, colours,
and drawings are satisfactory) are transfer prints ready for application to whatever range of pieces the pattern has been designed for.

There are two basic ways of transferring prints, whether litho or
screen, the one very much having superseded the other.

SIZED-DOWN This way of transferring prints is now largely obsolete but for many
TRANSFERS years it was the standard method. The ware was varnished and
dried and then with the backing paper removed the print was
carefully placed face downwards in the right position on the piece.
It was rubbed down and the transfer paper washed off as with
printed transfers. It was a complicated and unwieldy operation in
which absolute accuracy of application was essential.

SLIDE-OFF Now almost universal, this method is simpler, cleaner, and calls for
TRANSFERS less skill. The design has been printed onto a backing paper coated
with water-soluble glue, and over the top is printed a thin film of
flexible plastic (Collodion) which follows the outlines of the design
about $\frac{3}{32}''$ beyond it. When soaked in water the glue melts, the
design adheres to the film and can be slid off the backing paper onto
the surface to be decorated. More importantly, it can be shuffled
around on the surface until its position is right, and then it is

Application of a slide-off
transfer.

squeezed down using a small rubber kidney-shaped squeegee. One disadvantage of slide-off transfers is that because the film is non-adhesive it does not sit happily on very sharply curved or modelled surfaces. Warming the ware or the print will tend to obviate this but it does so only by softening the transfer film so that care has to be taken not to distort the design.

The stretching property of Collodion has both advantages and disadvantages. On the one hand it can be used to ease the fitting problem created by ware of various sizes, but on the other, its sensitivity to heat and pressure creates prints of variable size. Patterns that fit well in cold weather become stretched during application in warm weather and end up over size. Similarly, the girls applying transfers do not do so with equal pressure and as more pressure means more stretch this creates trouble.

Assuming that the print fits and has been squeegeed down in position, the piece is ready for firing unless a gold edge or some other kind of trim is needed, in which case it goes to the gilders first. I have not mentioned firing temperatures in this book because they vary too much from factory to factory. This is true of transfer print firings as well; the manufacturers will fit the colours in the print to the enamel-fire temperatures of the pottery.

The foregoing has been common to both kinds of transfer print; it is now necessary to make a distinction between them. They have nearly opposite characteristics and an understanding of these is quite essential to a designer deciding by which method a design is to be produced.

LITHOGRAPHY   This is a medium of great subtlety, good for obtaining soft gradations of tone or colour, bad at giving either very dark or very solid areas of colour. The reason for this is that the litho printing press prints in varnish, and powder colour is then dusted onto the transfer sheets giving a very light application of colour on any one printing. If a heavy colour is required, successive overprintings are necessary to build up to the desired strength, and this is both wasteful of printings and prone to break up in firing. However, the lightness of the printings makes it technically possible to print many colours, and some litho patterns currently in use have more than twenty. A more usual figure would be ten or twelve.

The characteristics of litho are hard to define. It has been used successfully, and less successfully, in many ways and to imitate many other media. The one thing that is certain is that more than any other ceramic decoration it offers a very wide scope to the designer.

Sections of transfer
showing the differing
characteristics of screen
print and litho.

SCREEN
PRINTING

Where lithography is complicated and subtle, screen printing is simple and direct. It gives flat solid areas of colour and while it is capable of intricate detail it is unsuitable for gradations of colour. The colour is printed directly onto the transfer sheet and this gives a heavy application.

The weight of application can be controlled but can never approach the lightness obtainable by litho; on most fired screen-print patterns the colour can be felt standing up proud of the glaze. This ability to print a heavy load of colour has been used, for instance, in successful imitation of raised paste. Seldom are more than six colours used in screen-print patterns, as much because of the character of the medium as for any other technical reasons.

The ability of screen printing to give flat large areas of plain colour has led to its use recently as a substitute for groundlaying on pieces where transferring presents no difficulty. Plate rims, for example, can easily be decorated this way with the additional advantage that gilding and other processes can be incorporated in the print. Where the bulk of a factory's production is in 'place setting' items the benefits are obvious.

Ideally screen-printed designs have to take advantage of the medium's hard edged, flat, bright simplicity. The tactile effect of the print is alo something that a designer can turn to advantage.

66

Until recently, the two branches of transfer printing were quite separate and carried on by different manufacturers. Designs had to be aimed at one or the other. Recently, industrial amalgamations and other factors have produced a few makers who can combine both techniques in one transfer. This has the advantage of being able to utilize the good points of both—solid colour and subtlety—but the tactile differences between the methods require careful handling.

CHAPTER 13 # Gilding

We could define gilding as the use of gold or silver in ceramic decoration and then it is a term that covers a number of activities and two quite distinct materials. Some of the activities have already been mentioned: the gold processes of both acid etching and raised paste are gilding, and painting, printing, and transfer printing can and do use gold. I therefore propose to use the term in its narrowest sense and the one that is more generally understood in the pottery industry. Gilding is finishing off, dressing up, putting on the trim. Nearly always a china plate is finished with a gold or silver edge. the cup with an edge, a line round the foot, and some work on the handle. This kind of finishing in metal, real or lustre, is common on white earthenware, china, and porcelain, and has been for two hundred years. It is less often found and less appropriate perhaps where coloured body or glazes are used.

The main distinction to be made is between the use of actual metal and of lustre.

METAL
GILDING
Metal gilding uses a metal sulphide resinate, usually of gold or platinum, held in suspension in a mixture of turps, ethyl glycol, and asphalt.

The brush deposits a mixture of metal and medium on the glaze and when enamel-fired the medium fires away leaving the metal particles embedded in the glaze surface. The surface of the metal when taken from the kiln is dull, the broken surface presented by small pieces of metal require burnishing before its metallic sheen is obtained. Ideally bloodstone is used: it flattens all the minute particles, unifies the surface, and gives a superb finish. But it is laborious, and on nearly all tableware the gilding is burnished with chamois leather and silver sand which does the job very well and much quicker but does not quite achieve the gleaming finish that the bloodstone does.

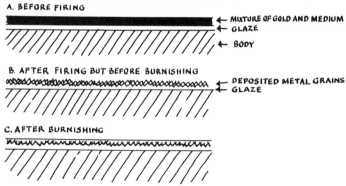

A. BEFORE FIRING

← MIXTURE OF GOLD AND MEDIUM
← GLAZE
← BODY

B. AFTER FIRING BUT BEFORE BURNISHING

← DEPOSITED METAL GRAINS
← GLAZE

C. AFTER BURNISHING

Above: Metallic gold edge being applied to a china plate.
Right: Enlarged section of ware surface. *From top:* applied mixture of gold and medium before firing; broken surface of deposited gold grains after firing; slick surface after burnishing.

In the heyday of gilding, around 1810, gilders at Derby, Worcester, and Spode's factory produced some superb pattern gilding, glorious brush strokes making magnificent scrolls, leaves and flourishes. Little of that scope is now allowed the gilder. Nine-tenths of the ware going through the gilding shop is circular, the bulk of it flat-ware requiring just an edge and gilded on a banding wheel. This is far from being a simple task, however, and a few minutes spent watching a good gilder at work will tell you more about his job than any description I could give. Line gilding has also to be carried out on many shapes other than circular ones: ovals,

68

squares, lozenge shapes—any shape the fertile brain of the designer produces the gilder has to edge. Once again, a few minutes spent with him might well be a moderating influence on a shape-designer! The degree of control necessary to put an even width edge around an octagonal plate on a banding wheel is considerable, but the only places where brush strokes are still used are on handles and knobs. A sad come-down from a glorious past, and while the expense rules out any real return to the days of free pattern gilding I have a personal feeling that gilding and the placing of gilding have become standardized without adequate reason.

LUSTRE GILDING This is an entirely different technique from the metal gilding of the last section. Here we are not using a metal in the raw state but rather a compound of that metal, usually a sulphide, which at firing temperature produces a metallic sheen. In some it is only faintly metallic as on the Sunderland lustre-ware of 1800—pink brush strokes with a faint pearly sheen to them. But at the same date convincingly metallic silver and copper lustres were being produced in Staffordshire, and it is the descendants of these that we use today. The effect is brilliant, glittering, and has led to the term 'liquid bright' which is general use for this type of gilding in the industry. The piece emerges from the kiln in its metallic glory requiring no burnishing or any further attention, in point of fact the less it is handled the better, for the finish tends to be somewhat vulnerable to abrasion.

The method of gilding is the same as for metal gilding except that its comparative cheapness allows liquid bright to be used rather more lavishly than pure metal. This is unfortunate, as *en masse* its effect tends to be vulgar. The most successful use of liquid bright in the past was on brush stroke patterns often over a coloured glaze, and it might be a more profitable direction for this medium than the imitation of its more expensive cousins. It must be pointed out, however, that it can be and is used successfully and with taste as trim for litho and other patterns.

COLOUR GILDING This strange contradiction in terms comes about from the industry's definition of gilding referred to before.

What is meant is trim applied to ware in the same fashion as in metal—edges, lines, dashes, etc.—but carried out in a normal enamel colour. The method is exactly the same although the transparency of the colour makes for extra difficulty and consequently the cost is sometimes greater despite the cheaper material. It is a pleasant change from metal trim and pulls the best out of some patterns.

In this section I proposed to describe, in so far as that is possible, what the designer himself does. The previous sections have dealt with techniques of making and decorating that are essential for a designer to know in order that he may work intelligently with the factory. These techniques vary slightly from factory to factory but all are well defined and recognized. When we turn to the techniques used by the designer himself this is no longer true. Each designer will find methods to suit himself, and the factory he works in. All I shall attempt to do in this section is to suggest a few techniques that might prove helpful before more individual ways are found.

The section is divided into two chapters. The first is concerned with what might be termed the craft of designing, the second with other aspects of the job and the designer's approach to it.

CHAPTER 14 # Designing methods

SHAPES   However strongly one feels about 'drawing board' shapes, and they are my own pet aversion, there is little doubt that almost all ideas for tableware shapes find their first expression in some form of drawing. Drawing is quick, flexible, and expressive as a means of arriving at the feel of a shape or range of shapes. I believe, though, that as soon as this character or personality has been achieved on the flat one should immediately use the lathe to find out how it works in three dimensions. Sketch models of plaster can show very soon whether the qualities attractive in a drawing are in fact viable in three dimensions or are just graphic. Often the most successful way is to work backwards and forwards using drawings and models alternately. What happens on the lathe gives a different direction to the idea and shows new possibilities for the shape—possibilities that are most easily explored by further drawing. In turn this new drawing must be tried out in the solid, and so on until the final shape is arrived at. This combination of the immediacy and flexibility of drawing with the solidity and stimulus of turning, in a single creative process, is to me the most exciting and satisfying part of designing.

I refer throughout this section to turning on the lathe as the way to arrive at a plaster shape since this is by far the most widely used method, but of course other modelling techniques must be used when the particular piece demands them. Oval gravy boats, for instance, are best developed quite freely by modelling in clay until proportion and looks are right and then waste moulding and casting into plaster for cleaning up. Although very inaccurate, this model will give a fair idea of the finished piece and can be very helpful as a guide when producing the actual model by more painstaking methods.

Some designers prefer to do all this exploratory and creative work at the same size as the finished pot, others start from the beginning by working 'clay size' so that as soon as a solution is found it can be moulded immediately, without necessitating remodelling and possible loss of effect. I personally find it difficult to judge new shapes unless they are the final fired size and I can rely on the shape being repeatable when the design is finalized. This method has the advantage that a fired size sketch model is available when the design is to be submitted for approval. A whole range of shapes can be shown in this way, even more convincingly if hollowed out, and without incurring any mould-making expense.

While there is little doubt that plaster sketch models done in this way are a more effective way of presenting new shapes than by drawing, there are dangers. One is the unsympathetic nature of plaster as a material. Sketch models made from it, while accurately conveying the shape of the final piece, are totally different from it in weight, colour, and texture. Trivial though this might seem, I have known an uneasiness about these qualities to prejudice the fate of a design. The person to whom designs are submitted, though normally skilled in assessing such things as the sales potential and factory practicability of new items, seldom finds it easy to visualize the final appearance from sketches and sketch models. For designers accustomed to making such mental projections this is difficult to understand; but it is definitely a factor to be considered. To some extent this problem can be eased by painting, varnishing, or otherwise faking the plaster to more closely resemble the final pot.

Another more serious problem attends the use of plaster sketch models and this applies more particularly to porcelain and bone china shapes. However experienced a designer is he cannot ever predict with certainty exactly how a shape will behave in the kiln. This kiln factor can work both ways. Often a shape will sag unpleasantly after firing, necessitating modification of the model, even reconsideration of the whole shape. But almost as often the firing will underline some desirable quality in the modelling perhaps hitherto unnoticed by the designer which can influence his view of the whole range of shapes. By submitting shapes in plaster sketch form without any firing tests on them the designer runs the double risk of committing himself to shapes that are difficult to pot or fire and of missing possible help from the kiln.

As a student I helped design a range of bone china shapes for a well known company, and with my fellow designer produced a complete set of plaster sketch models for every item, painstakingly hollowed out and very impressive. The range was accepted and I remember being puzzled by the anger of the modellers who were to work from our splendid models. By presenting them with absolutely cut and dried shapes to reproduce we had denied them any room to manoeuvre and had set them a lot of very difficult problems. Some of the shapes proved impossible to reproduce and some of the others still, after over twelve years, make me wince at their 'plaster feel'.

I now make a point, when producing a range of shapes, of getting the feel of the character by the drawing–modelling–drawing process described earlier. Then, as soon as the shape is at all defined, I model a key piece—a teapot or coffee pot usually—get it moulded, cast, fired, and glazed in the normal way. Usually the lessons learned from this affect the design of other pieces in the range; problems can be spotted and avoided; qualities can be assessed and modelled for. For presentation one has a finished piece which apart from being visually more impressive than plaster models is also invaluable for demonstrating pouring characteristics, capacity, and so on. The rest of the pieces, shown either in drawing or model form become much more believable to salesmen and directors when seen alongside one finished piece.

It should be emphasized that this sequence is one that I personally have found workable, but it has been evolved as much from the methods and characteristics of the factory that employed me as from my own preferences. Other designers, other factories, will work in totally different ways and God forbid it should be otherwise! Designing methods, unlike potting and decorating methods, are entirely personal; the only criteria I would suggest are that they should give the designer maximum control over all stages.

PATTERN While the general principles suggested in the previous section certainly apply to designing patterns as much as shapes, the techniques used for patterns by a designer are much more varied.

As with shape, some designers work almost entirely on paper, developing and refining a pattern until it is in its final form, getting it produced by the appropriate method and only applying it to the pot then. Others work backwards and forwards from paper to pot, getting the pattern onto the ware in some form however sketchily from the beginning and altering and refining the pattern as much on the pot as on the paper. It is even possible to develop ideas for litho decoration without any drawing on paper at all. Recently a fellow designer of mine, interested in the effect of watercolour painting on the porcelain surface, and disappointed at the loss of this quality on paper, submitted the final design on porcelain. The litho manufacturer reproduced the fresh and spontaneous quality of the design with some sensitivity and the result is a pattern that would not have been half as effective if the normal method of submitting the design on paper or card had been followed.

I have referred, and shall refer again to pattern designing mainly in relation to on-glaze litho and screen-print transfers because these are by far the most common methods met with and they are the ones with which I am most familiar.

In the shape section I dwelt at some length on the methods of presentation of designs, because I consider this to be a very important side of the designer's trade. If this is true of shape design it is even more true of pattern design. Not only do proposed designs have to be seen and approved by directors, sales managers, decorating managers, and other people on the factory itself, but often they are also shown to people in the retail trade, and occasionally they are even used in market research. When the decision on the adoption of new patterns was entirely an internal matter and probably involved only a few people, it was normal and quite satisfactory for designs to be submitted and assessed on paper. But increasingly the tendency now is to gather expert, and inexpert, advice from outside the factory from the trade and from the general public. Drawings of patterns are of little validity there, and increasingly the designer has to produce the patterns on the ware itself, usually on a dinner plate. Because by far the largest number of such patterns are ultimately to be produced by either screen print or litho transfer, and because to get a pattern produced by either of these means, even in trial or proof form, is costly, the designer has to find ways of imitating these media satisfactorily on the factory itself. This often affects the way he develops his pattern ideas.

In the old way, the designer develops his pattern idea on paper until he considers it is satisfactory and then he presents it for approval as a drawing, probably in gouache and on card. When the decision is made to put the pattern into production he produces a very careful gouache drawing of a section of the pattern on a paper fitting, usually for a ten-inch plate, and passes this to the litho manufacturer for him to 'prove' as a litho transfer. Because of the difficulty of satisfactorily rendering opaque gouache effect in transparent ceramic colours the first litho proof is usually a disappointment to the designer. At this point he has to decide how far he should insist that the original drawing is exactly followed by the litho manufacturer, remembering that it is this drawing that his own superiors are familiar with. He may have to accept that it is impossible to reproduce exactly and that the first proof litho must be used as a starting point, improved and refined until it is satisfactory. The size of the problem depends on how much difference there is between drawing and proof, and this can be kept to a minimum by knowledge of ceramic colours and sensitive drawing on the part of the designer, and care on the part of the litho man. With experience, the translation to litho can be accomplished quite satisfactorily and the pattern can even gain from it. However, the young designer will often find himself very disappointed in the first proofs of a new pattern and embarrassed by the discrepancy when salesmen, directors, and the like are expecting the ware to look just like his beautifully presented drawing.

A solution to this problem has already been hinted at. The pressure on a designer to produce finished pieces of decorated ware without incurring the considerable expense of litho proving, has forced him to effect the translation to ceramic colour himself. This can be done by developing the pattern up to its final stage as before, on paper, and then reproducing the finished drawing on pot by hand-painting or groundlaying or whatever method seems to give the closest result. There are no better ways of learning what effects, what colours, are inappropriate or even impossible in on-glaze decoration than by doing this. The only problem is that often the makeshift decorating methods, at first devised only to produce sample pieces, start to suggest changes in the pattern itself. How much the media are allowed to have their say is, of course, up to the designer, but it seems wise, if they are to have any say at all, that the adjustment should happen early rather than late in the designing process. So, increasingly, designers start working in ceramic colours on pot as soon as the pattern idea is defined and long before they find themselves hamstrung by a 'presentation drawing'. The to and fro character of this kind of designing has much in common with the similar stage in shape designing when work on paper is alternated with work on the lathe. Similarly, in pattern designing it is necessary to return to paper to develop the idea; and, in spite of the instance given at the beginning of this section, it is almost always best to carry out on paper the designs that are to be passed to litho firms. But they will be paper designs informed by ceramic experience and accompanied by ceramic samples.

One particular kind of drawing for reproduction should perhaps be mentioned here. Monochrome patterns for screen print, small in scale but precise and intricate in character, are often rather difficult to draw at that size. The answer is to scale the pattern up to a more convenient size and to draw it in black on white regardless of the intended final colour. The screen-print manufacturer will in any case have to transfer the drawing to his screen photographically and can adjust the scale then. The large size of the drawing ensures accuracy and the black and white helps to retain clarity.

SAMPLING
METHODS
These will depend a lot on the designer's preferences and on what skills and facilities are available at the factory he works for. These are a few useful methods I have used.

Engraving. If the factory has an engraver or an engraving shop, that is a great advantage for the designer. Engraving can be used to give outline prints for almost any kind of pattern and for litho or screen print. It can be used as a heavy outline to imitate screen printing or as the finest of fine lines printed in a pale colour, as a valuable guide to hand-painting, when imitating the soft effect of litho. The engraver need only cut a small section of a design—one complete motif is usually enough. The designer will probably want to put the print down himself; he will not mind the inconvenience of putting it down in many small pieces as this gives him more chance to shuffle the pattern about. Apart from the more obvious advantages that the use of print has when sampling patterns, there is the quality that a good engraver will give to any pattern, a quality impossible to obtain on paper.

Etching. A passable imitation of engraving, when that method is not available, can be gained by etching the design on copper. This of course will bring to the design quite a different set of qualities from those resulting from engraving, and again these can be turned to advantage.

These two methods are used mostly to give an outline to the pattern to be sampled, although they can also give both tone and texture, but unless the pattern is to be entirely monochromatic most colours must be added in subsequent firings in one or more of the following ways.

Painting. If the pattern being sampled is ultimately intended for litho production then the softness and gradation of colour typical of litho can only be successfully imitated by hand painting, and very good painting at that. Unless a very skilled and obliging painter is available it behoves the designer to learn the job himself.

Groundlaying. While the gradations of litho can only be imitated by painting, the flat solid colours of screen printing can best be rendered by colour applied by oiling and dusting. Although a laborious method, very convincing 'screen-print' patterns can be sampled by groundlaying small areas and cleaning off around the pattern, usually with a printed outline as a guide. Colours have to be added singly and the piece fired after each additional colour.

Flat colour screen print. Screen-print manufacturers produce sheets of flat colour on transfer screen and as an alternative to the above method shapes can be cut out from these and applied to the ware. The method does have the advantage that with care more than one colour can be added at a time. However, unless the designer is a virtuoso on the scissors, the patterns obtained this way are necessarily simple. The 'paper-cut' quality brought to the pattern by this method is also not always appropriate.

These, then, are some of the methods that can be used to produce sample decorations and also, as I have suggested, to develop the design. There are others which may well be found useful: colour banding, for instance, or aerographing colour through stencils. The important point is that these means are not seen merely as imitating litho or screen-print transfers, although they do this very well; more than this, they are ways of developing ceramic decorations in ceramic terms and they give a quality or even new direction to the litho or screen print in which the pattern is finally produced.

Up to now, the pattern has been thought of almost entirely in terms of the ten-inch plate, and this is the form in which most tableware patterns are developed. Often during the development and the sampling stages the designer will sketch out the pattern on other pieces in the range—particularly on the teacup and saucer for example—but detailed consideration of the whole range is deferred until the pattern is accepted for production.

The designer will usually want to have a full range in white glost of the required pieces in order to decide on the disposition of the pattern on each piece. This is a relatively important decision: the position and weight of pattern on a piece is seen by a potential customer long before colour or drawing or style are evident.

When the areas of decoration on each piece have been decided the next stage is to 'fit up' the pattern. This is a relatively boring job and I shall not pretend it is otherwise. Some designers duck it altogether, sending a range of ware to the litho manufacturers and letting him get on with it, and while this to me seems a bit too easy it has its advantages. One of them is that you have someone else to blame when the litho doesn't fit! However, we will assume that the designer is to do his own fits, and, although this does involve him in a lot of tricky and relatively unrewarding work, at least he has control of his own pattern right the way through from conception to production.

FITTINGS   Unless the pattern is a spray or sprig type pattern where small motifs are applied singly to the various pots in the range, it will be necessary to take paper patterns or 'fits' of the areas to be decorated on all the pieces. Almost all surfaces of ceramic tableware are curved, and it is to make sure that litho transfers, which are printed on flat paper, are drawn in such a way that they fall in exactly the right position when wrapped around these curves, that these fittings are required.

Methods of taking fittings can vary, but are generally similar to the following. Let us assume for example, that the pattern is to be in a wide band near the top of a coffee pot, ending either side of the upper handle terminal. First, two parallel and horizontal lines are drawn around the pot marking the upper and lower limits of the pattern. Next, a sheet of tissue paper is wrapped around the relevant area of the pot, and is gradually cut and refitted until it fits smoothly to the pot surface between the drawn lines. With the tissue held firmly by dabs of gum the lines and position of handle terminals are traced carefully. The tissue is removed and these marks are transferred to a sheet of cartridge paper where they show the limits within which the pattern must be arranged.

If the pot is circular in section then the upper and lower limits projected on paper will be true arcs and can be trued up with compasses. The nearer the pot shape is to a cylinder the nearer straight the lines will be, while obviously the more tapered the shape the more sharply curved they become. If the pot profile is sharply convex or concave at the point where the fit is to be taken it will make things more difficult. A useful tip in such cases is to draw on the pot a line half-way between the limit lines and parallel to them and first fit the tissue to that. On convex pots the tissue will crease either side of this line as it is smoothed out to the limit lines; make sure that it does this evenly on either side. If it is concave, then vertical cuts will be necessary along each edge of the paper to get it down. In both these cases it must be remembered that the litho transfer will tend to behave as the tissue, and will either crease or split when being rubbed down unless some provision in the form of deep indents along the upper and lower edges is made. As a check on the accuracy of the fitting, it is prudent to cut each one out again in cartridge paper and re-apply to the pot to satisfy oneself that no innaccuracy has crept in during the tracing. This done, the cartridge paper fits are used as templates and they are drawn out again on sheets of paper for the pattern to be drawn to them. Before that can be started we must decide how to divide up the fits.

Few pieces in the range are suitable for application of the litho in one long piece. The number of pieces into which a fit is divided depends on several factors. A continuous border pattern, for instance, is usually applied to a ten-inch plate in three equal pieces, because that makes both for easy handling and application and also because it enables a large number of pieces to be packed onto the litho sheet. But, depending on the pattern, five-piece, four-piece, two-piece and even whole circle, one-piece applications are sometimes used. It is wise to consult the decorating manager on this question and indeed his help is invaluable at all stages of pattern fitting.

PROVING   A finished drawing of a section of the pattern usually fitted for a ten-inch plate is now sent to the transfer manufacturer for him to 'prove'. Sometimes when different sizes of work or a wide variety of motifs will be needed on the range it is as well to prove extra pieces. The teacup and saucer is often included on the proof sheet, and sometimes even the complete place setting of ten-, seven- and five-inch plates and teacup and saucer, to give a representative range of sizes and motifs. But the main point of proving is to get the colour and drawing of a pattern right without the expense of doing the whole range, so the proof sheet must not get too overloaded or proving becomes both lengthy and expensive. It is unusual for first proofs to be entirely satisfactory—the manufacturer usually has to have two or more shots before getting a correct balance of colours—but however faulty they are, the proof sheets have one important use: particularly if several items have been proved, the sheets are useful for cutting up and piecing together on the whole range. This gives the designer a much more accurate idea of how the pattern will look than any drawing, and enables him to design freely with existing print on each piece.

When the arrangement has been finalized on everything it is

transferred accurately to the appropriate fit. Tracing from the ware sometimes helps at this stage. It is not necessary to do finished drawings of the pattern for every piece; this would involve the designer in needlessly repetitive work. If new work, not included on the proof sheet, is needed, then this should be properly drawn out, but all work taken from the proof sheet can be indicated either by outline drawing or by actual print from the proof sheets. I have found the latter most effective; it shows exactly what is wanted and also indicates clearly where new work has been added by drawing.

It is as well to remember when laying out the fits that the cover coat screen used on litho and screen transfers is inclined to stretch particularly in hot weather, and it is advisable to allow for this by keeping the pattern short of the ends of each fitted area. It is difficult to specify the exact allowance as it depends on many factors, but about a quarter of an inch stretch in a foot length of screen is reasonable. It is always better to allow too much rather than too little as the fits can be stretched by warming and extra pressure on the squeegee, but overlaps are impossible to conceal.

BLACK
IMPRESSIONS
When all fittings are complete they are handed to the manufacturer and he produces from them a full set of 'black impressions'. These are outline prints of all the pattern fittings in transfer form and are produced as a safeguard to make sure all the fittings actually do fit the ware before the complicated and very expensive colour printing is put in hand. It is best to let the litho foreman try out the black impressions; he will soon tell you their short-comings. Alterations are submitted as before and come back as new black impressions to be tried once more. Only when everything fits and handles perfectly will the printing of the litho edition start, and then, of course, only when the colour and drawing have been finalized on proof sheets.

In closing this section which has been concerned entirely with the designer's job in preparing designs for production, I would like to emphasize that his work is far from over. Particularly in shape design and to some extent also in pattern the designer has 'servicing' work to do on designs already in production. Shapes that are proving difficult to make or to fire, shapes switched to new making methods, additions to the range, new techniques—problems such as these constantly arise and a large proportion of the designer's time is spent talking to managers trying to ease difficulties on existing pieces without spoiling their appearance.

Personally, I welcome this continual involvement with factory business. Close observation of a shape or pattern in production and of the kind of things that go wrong with it, is an excellent way of guarding against similar mistakes next time. It gives the designer the opportunity also to get to know the people as well as the machines that produce ware from his designs. Designing pottery is not a cold-blooded question-and-answer activity; the designer gets involved with his own designs. He has created some pieces which still give him a feeling of satisfaction years after their introduction. Similarly there are ones which were never quite resolved, although in trouble-free production perhaps for even longer. The maker on the bench has his favourites as well, and for equally valid reasons: it is no bad thing to listen to them sometimes.

During the preceding sections I have talked of processes and have implied that they often suggest design ideas. Potters generally spend all their working lives in the industry; they think about their jobs, take a pride in them, and are generous with help when they get to know you. Good design ideas grow from the factory—from the men as well as from the machines—if the designer is alive to them.

CHAPTER 15 # Designing approach

This book has been about the factory aspect of a designer's work, the processes of manufacture, the ways they can be used, their limitations, and their ability to stimulate design. In a very involved and complicated way it is just the same as a stone-carver describing his tools and techniques. But stone carving is not just tools and how to use them, nor is pottery designing; what I have described so far are just the means of realizing ideas.

In turning now to some other sides of the designer's job I am very conscious that this is dangerous ground. The processes and methods of the industry are complicated but they are not controversial: the attitudes in this section *are* personal, and very much open to question.

The tableware industry, like any other, can only survive if it can sell its products at a profit. The aptness of the product to the market is as much the designer's concern as its production viability. He has to be as much alive to the market and its needs as to the factory and its capabilities; for while the latter governs how a design is produced the former dictates what is designed.

Design ideas, of course come from many sources, the factory itself for instance (as I have suggested), from textiles, carvings, flowers, in fact the whole visual world; but to be of use these have to be seen in relation to the market. The designer must be aware of design trends both in his own industry and in others; he must know what is selling, where, and at what price, and what is not selling and why. He must be able to aim patterns and shapes at particular sections of the market and he must know what his company's competitors are doing. All of this means a great deal of outward-looking designing as well as the inward-looking stressed in the preceding pages. It also means time spent in stores and a close working relationship with the sales force.

Human relationships, in fact, play a major part in the job. An ability to get on with people, to understand their points of view, and to explain one's own honestly and lucidly is a valuable asset to a designer. This ability, apart from making his own working life more pleasant, enables him to gather information easily, information that he needs from both salesmen and craftsmen. As well as the information and help that the factory can give him, he needs from the salesmen knowledge that would be difficult to gain by himself. He needs to know what buyers think of a particular pattern, what the reaction to an alteration in handle shape has been, why a certain line hasn't sold—hundreds of little facts and opinions that will help in future designing. He has, of course, *formal* contacts with both factory and sales people, but unless he can forge *personal* links with both sides, his supply of information is likely to be thin and dry.

Human relationships are important, too, when we consider the designer as a salesman. For salesman he sometimes has to be. The finest piece of design work, combining huge sales potential with ease of production, visually exciting and technically a breakthrough, is quite useless unless the factory can be persuaded to produce it. This is one reason why such emphasis was laid in the previous section on the presentation aspects of designing, on sketch models, mock-ups, sample plates and so on. All these are very important, but usually even more important is the designer himself talking about the design, explaining, defending, and advocating. It might be said that this is not his job, that what he should do is complete his work, make as good a presentation as possible, let the design speak for itself, and let the powers that be take it or leave it. I think that this is a fundamentally wrong view of designing; but there is a more practical objection. The people assessing the design will tend to leave it. They will reason, understandably, that if the designer believes so little in his own design that he will not speak out for it, then he cannot expect them to have confidence in it.

Designing is very much, it seems to me, concerned with involvement: with the means of production, with the market and the means of selling it; and not least the designer's involvement with the thing he designs. There is a time on every design project when the designer commits himself to a particular design solution. Quite possibly it will be no more than a vague idea to be modified by all kinds of factors. On the other hand it may be complete, neat, satisfying all the conditions of the job. But in either case the decision is of the utmost importance to the designer. From that moment he is committed to nursing the idea through design and factory stages towards production. At every point he will have to meet arguments from people who want to alter it or stop it. If it were a little more tapered, the mould-makers suggest, it would come from a one-piece mould; if it were lower, the china manager pleads, it would fit this machine, and so on. All through the factory and from salesmen too, come objections, suggestions, observations, and all have to be listened to, some are used to modify the design, most have to be rejected and the rejection explained. I do not want to over-emphasize the crusading aspect of designing but in order to be honest the designer must believe in his designs and in order to be effective he must be prepared to fight for them, no less in the boardroom than on the factory floor.

Glossary

Acid etching. A process in which a design is etched on the glaze surface to enhance subsequent gilding. See chap 11.

Aniseed oil. Medium used in on-glaze painting.

Back stamp. Trademark, maker's name, etc., printed or impressed on back of ware.

Banding. Application of bands of colour, by brush, to revolving pots. See chaps. 7 and 9.

Bat. Pancake of clay.

Bisque. Term used to describe ceramic after firing and before glaze, or glost firing.

Black impressions. Outline transfers of a litho or screen-print design, submitted by the manufacturer in order that fits can be accurately checked.

Block mould. Mould made directly from initial model.

Bloodstone. Used in burnishing, to obtain very bright finish on gold decoration.

Bomb. Term sometimes used for profile tool in roller making.

Body-stain. Colour introduced into the clay itself for decorative effect.

Boss. Pad used in groundlaying. See chap. 10.

Bossing. Cleaning copper plate during printing process. See chap. 7.

Can. Cylindrical shaped coffee cup.

Case mould (master mould). Positive mould made from block mould and from which working moulds can be produced.

Chatter. Fault in plaster turning. See chap. 1.

China (bone). Type of porcelain containing large percentage of bone ash.

Chum or chuck. Lathe attachment for holding pots during turning process.

Clay size. Size of ware as made, prior to drying or firing shrinkage.

Claying down. Method of attaching models or pots to horizontal surface—usually wheelheads—using a small roll of plastic clay.

Collodion. Plastic film used in slide-off transfers. See chap. 12.

Contraction. Shrinkage due to firing or drying of ware.

Copper. Copper plate used in producing printed designs.

Cottle. Coil of lino used to retain plaster while it is setting.

Crawling. A glaze fault. See chap. 8.

Crazing. Minute cracking of glaze, sometimes induced intentionally, but more usually a fault.

Dabber. Wooden tool used in printing.

Deflocculant. Chemical used to increase fluidity of slip.

Die pressing. Little used making method. See chap. 4.

Double-cast. Form of casting where moulds form both inside and outside of the piece. See chap 4.

Driers. Drying chambers used to dry either moulds or ware.

Earthenware. Porous ceramic usually made from refined clays. Must be glazed to hold liquid.

Engraving. Most common method of preparing copper plates. See chap. 11.

Facing up. Producing an impermeable surface on plaster by use of soft soap, in order to ensure separation.

Fat-oil. Medium used in on-glaze painting.

Fettling. Term used in making to describe final cleaning up prior to firing.

Fired size. Final size of ware, usually compared with clay size in order to determine shrinkage.

Fittings. Pattern arrangement on various pieces in a range.

Flat-ware. Plates, dishes, etc., as distinct from hollow-ware, teapots, etc.

Gilding. Application of final decorative trim, usually in gold. See chap. 13.

Glost. Glazed or glazing, hence glost kiln, glost ware, etc.

Gouache. 'Poster' type of watercolour.

Graver. Tool used in engraving.

Groundlaying. Method of applying flat on-glaze colour. See chap. 10.

Hand making. A method of making irregular flat-ware by pressing.

Hollow-ware. Bowls, cups, jugs, teapots, etc., as distinct from flat-ware, plates, etc.

In-glaze decoration. A method of decorating in under-glaze colour on a fired glaze surface, fired a second time through the glost kiln. See chap. 7.

Jasper. A stone-ware pioneered by Wedgwood using white sprigged relief decoration on coloured ground. See chap. 5.

Jiggering. Making method. See chap. 3.

Jolleying. As above.

Lathe turning. Principal method of plaster model making.

Leather-hard. Term used to describe partially dried pots.

Litho (lithography). Main method of producing transfers for ceramic decoration. See chap. 12.

Lustre. Type of gilding. See chap. 13.

Lute. Method of fixing together clay pieces, using slip.

Natch. Means of ensuring positive location of mould parts. Usually small round indentations and projections.

Natch knife. Hooked tool used for cutting natches.

Palette knife. Flexible tool used in grinding and mixing ceramic colour.

Piece mould. Mould made in more than one piece.

Photo etching. Method of preparing printing copper plates—less used than engraving.

Pitcher. Fired clay, usually earthenware, sometimes used for making moulds.

Place setting. Three sizes of plate 10″, 7″, and 5″, and teacup and saucer, make up one place setting.

Polychrome. Multi-coloured, as distinct from monochrome.

Porcelain. Vitreous, white, translucent ceramic.

Pottery. Porous ceramic made from unrefined clay. Must be glazed in order to hold liquid.

Pouring hole. Hole in casting moulds necessary for filling and emptying.

Pressing. Making method, see chap. 4.

Printing. Method of decorating pottery with one-colour transfers from copper plates.

Print and enamel. As above, but with added colours applied by brush.

Profile. Chamfered metal plate of appropriate section used in jiggering and jolleying. See chap. 3.

Proof sheets. Trial transfers of litho or screen print. See chap. 14.

Pug (pug-mill). Machine used to prepare clay for making processes. It extrudes clay in the form of pug-rolls.

Punch. Tool used in engraving.

Raised paste. Used in gold decoration, usually printed. See chap. 11.

Rigget. Channel on press moulds designed to hold surplus clay squeezed out from pressing.

Roller making. See chap. 3.

Roller printing. See chap. 7.

Sagger. Container made from coarse clay in which pots are placed to protect them from the flames during firing.

Salt-glaze stone ware. Type of ware glazed by volatilization of salt introduced during firing.

Screen print. Methods of producing transfer prints. See chap. 12.

Seam. Junction between two parts of a mould, hence seam line, the mark left by this join on the cast.

Self-scrapping. Automatic removal of surplus clay in jolleying process. See chap. 3.

Setting up. Term used in block-mould making to describe preliminary work before plaster is poured.

Sgraffito. Incised decoration. See chap. 5.

Sized-down. A type of transfer print. See chap. 12.

Slide-off. Type of transfer print alternative to above. See chap. 12.

Slip. Clay mixed with water to a pourable consistency.

Slip-casting. Making method. See chap. 4.

Slug. Lump of plastic clay sliced by wire from the pug-roll.

Slurry. Thick, creamy mixture of clay and water, used for attaching handles, etc. to pots.

Snip. Pouring lip of a jug.

Spare. Plaster extensions to a model added to facilitate mould-making.

Sprigging. Relief decoration, taken from separate moulds and applied to the pot or model.

Spring. Term used in modelling to describe slight doming, sometimes necessary on flat surfaces.

Squeegee. Used in application of slide-off transfer prints.

Sticking-up area. Points of attachment where casts are joined together.

Stone-ware. Vitreous, non-translucent ceramic.

Swell. Slight expansion of plaster upon setting.

Tipping. Raised colour or paste applied by brush.

Towing. In fettling, tow is often used as a gentle abrasive on the dry clay.

Transfer prints. Prints produced either by litho or screen-print method for pottery decoration.

Under-glaze decoration. This is applied before glazing, and is fired, together with the glaze, through the glost kiln.

Whirler. A vertical lathe with heavy, plaster wheelhead.

Working moulds. Moulds used in production.

Wreathing. Fault in plaster turning. See chap. 11. Also refers to similar fault in slip-casting. See chap. 4.

Index